© Hodder Children's Books 2006

Published in Great Britain in 2006 by Hodder Children's Books

Editor: Isabel Thurston
Design by Fiona Webb
Cover design: Hodder Children's Books

2

ISBN-10: 0 340 91732 6
ISBN-13: 978 0 340 91732 9

Printed by Bookmarque Ltd, Croydon, Surrey

The paper and board used in this paperback by Hodder Children's Books are natural recyclable products made from wood grown in sustainable forests. The manufacturing processes conform to the environmental regulations of the country of origin.

Hodder Children's Books
a division of Hachette Children's Books
338 Euston Road
London NW1 3BH

CONTENTS

INTRODUCTION

So you think you know all about the weird
and wonderful, amazing and amusing
Discworld? Reckon you can summon up all
the moments of magic and madness that
Rincewind, Mort, Death, Susan and the
hundreds of other incredible characters
encounter? Then this unofficial quizbook,
not to be found in Unseen University's library,
is for you! It contains over 1000 questions
culled from the thirty *Discworld* novels –
from *The Colour of Magic* right through to
Thud! Each novel gets its own dedicated quiz,
and at the end of the book there are also five
quizzes with miscellaneous questions about
all the novels: the first is as simple as Cut Me
Own Throat Dibbler's business plans, the rest
are tougher than a steak at Harga's House of
Ribs.

About the author

Clive Gifford is an award-winning author
of books for children and young adults
including *The Cosmic Toaster*, *Pants Attack!*
and *Crimebusters*. He is also the author of the
So You Think You Know quiz books including
titles on *Narnia*, *The Simpsons*, *The Da Vinci
Code* and *Dr Who*. Clive can be contacted at
his website: www.clivegifford.co.uk

THE COLOUR OF MAGIC

1 Do Great Nef tribesmen often wear turbans on their heads, knees or elbows?

2 Tethis rescues Twoflower and what other character?

3 Was Laolith, Liartes or Larrabold a brother of Liessa Wyrmbidder?

4 The Circumference is found at: Discworld's Hub, the edge of the Rim or surrounding Ankh-Morpork?

5 What is the name, beginning with the letter B, of one of the giant elephants that stands on A'Tuin's back?

6 What number between one and ten do sensible wizards never mention?

7 Zlorf Flannelfoot is president of the Guild of: Plumbers, Philosophers or Assassins?

8 Dunmanifestin is the home of: old wizards, the Disc's gods or disgraced ghosts?

9 Liessa Wyrmbidder rode what sort of creature as her mount?

 10 What colour is the sword, Kring, wielded by Hrun the Barbarian?

 11 Is the name of one of the four elephants on which Discworld rests: Great A'Tuin, Great A'Rango or Great T'Phon?

 12 How many hundred days does it take for Discworld to complete a revolution?

 13 Is Widdershins: a dwarf in *The Truth*, a direction that Discworld turns in or the butler of Moist von Lipwig?

 14 Who battled Bel-Shamharoth?

 15 How many eyes does Twoflower have: one, two, three or four?

 16 Is Black Oroogu, Sumtri or Vanglemesht a language with no nouns and only one adjective?

 17 Who was the original owner of the Luggage who appears in this and a number of other *Discworld* books?

18 What is the name of the giant, upside-down mountain?

19 The lands of the Hub are: desert, icy or float 100 metres above the Disc's surface?

20 Is Zephyrus the god of chocolate, bad luck or slight breezes?

21 Bel-Shamharoth was also known as Fate, Death or the Soul-Eater?

22 Are Captain Eightpanther's Travellers' Digestives pulled out of the Luggage by Rincewind, Granny Weatherwax or Twoflower?

23 Which two of the following are dragons: Laolith, Psepha, Stren Withel or Dactylos?

24 Who does Liessa Wyrmbidder instruct to kill both of her brothers, and in return she will marry him?

25 Whose name is the first word Death speaks in *The Colour of Magic*?

26 What number between one and ten is the number of Bel-Shamharoth?

27 The Sorca people in *The Colour of Magic* are known for building dams and structures to capture: rain, magic or sunlight?

 28 Were the people of Krull, the Agatean Empire or Klatch the first to peer over the rim of Discworld and see Great A'Tuin?

 29 Dactylos built the metal warriors that guard the tomb of Pitchiu. What injury did he suffer as a result?

 30 What is the name, beginning with the letter J, of one of the giant elephants that stands on A'Tuin's back?

THE LIGHT FANTASTIC

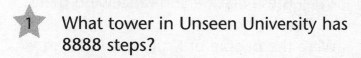

1   What tower in Unseen University has 8888 steps?

2   Olaf Quimby II was killed by: a rogue spell, a poet, a troll or a shower of ornamental frogs?

3   Who is Cohen the Barbarian planning to marry?

4   Is a Thaum, an Omm or a Wand-Watt a unit of magical strength?

5   Which wizard stole the Octavo and locked the other wizards in a room?

6   Which character is 87 years old in the book and has a bad back?

7   Herrena the Henna-Haired Harridan is sent to capture which wizard?

8   Was Kwartz the troll's wife called Granite, Opal, Slate or Beryl?

9 Which member of Unseen University did the Luggage swallow?

10 Who is the first person Rincewind meets at Death's house?

11 Does the Bumper Fun Grimoire, the Octavo or the Necrotelicomnicon allegedly contain the one original joke left in the universe?

12 Are there 12, 24, 32 or 64 signs of the zodiac in Discworld?

13 As Belafon is transporting a giant rock to a druids' stone circle, does he describe his job as a sculptor, a priest or a computer hardware consultant?

14 Who, at the start of the book, is second in command of the wizards, only drinks water and doesn't smoke?

15 Rincewind meets Twoflower and enters a gingerbread cottage in: Ankh-Morpork, Klatch or the Forest of Skund?

16 Who swings Death's scythe at Rincewind only for the Luggage to catch the blade?

17 Galder's spell to bring back Rincewind instead brings back: Twoflower, Cohen the Barbarian or the Luggage?

 18 Does Rincewind, Trymon, Death or Twoflower tell the wizards that all the spells of the Octavo have to be told, otherwise the Disc will be destroyed?

 19 Who arrives on the Luggage and stops Rincewind from falling off the tower at Unseen University?

 20 On what device with handlebars do Rincewind and Twoflower escape the wizards in the gingerbread cottage?

 21 Which one of the following is not a sign of the zodiac in Discworld: Mubbo the Hyaena, the Vase of Tulips or the Celestial Halibut?

 22 Is Greyhald Spold the youngest, oldest, most powerful or most insane of all the wizards?

 23 Who insists on interrupting the ceremony in which the druids are about to sacrifice Bethan?

24 Is Ysabell, Twoflower or Rincewind playing cards with Death, Famine, War and Pestilence at Death's house?

 25 Is the River Ankh, Skund or Smarl the longest river in Discworld?

 26 Lackjaw the jeweller provides Cohen the Barbarian with a set of diamond teeth. Is Lackjaw a druid, dwarf, golem or vampire?

 27 The gods of Discworld are in a long war with the Ice Giants over what item that the Ice Giants did not return?

 28 Did the creatures of the Dungeon Dimensions enter Discworld through Trymon, Rincewind, Twoflower or Cohen the Barbarian?

 29 One Thaum is the amount of magic necessary to create how many billiard balls?

 30 Which one of the following is not a title of Galder Weatherwax's: Lord Imperial of the Sacred Staff, Eighth Level Ipsissimus or Illustrious Mage of the Five Kingdoms?

LORDS AND LADIES

1. Is the Duck Man rejected from or let in to the Beggars' Guild?

2. The village of Bad Ass is in which country: Lancre, Sto Lat or Klatch?

3. Diamanda is hit in the shoulder by an arrow fired by: witches, elves or the City Watch?

4. Ridcully turns the bandit chieftan into what sort of Halloween vegetable?

5. What creatures cover Granny Weatherwax, helping to bring her back to life?

6. Which one of the following is a witch: Lady Sybil Ramkin, Polly Perks or Magrat Garlick?

7. The problem with the Lancre shilling as currency is that it is: invisible, weighs almost a kilo per coin or smells like a skunk?

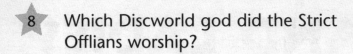

8 Which Discworld god did the Strict Offlians worship?

9 Is Lancre a land of deserts, mountains or plains?

10 How many dollars does the coachman charge to take Ridcully and the others to Lancre?

11 Who is Diamanda's opponent in the witches' staring contest in Lancre?

12 Elves have greenish-blue blood: true or false?

13 In her will, did Granny Weatherwax's leave her bed and her broomstick to Nanny Ogg or Magrat Garlick?

14 Can you name two of the staff members of Unseen University who travel to Lancre for the wedding of King Verence II?

15 Which two of the following claims are on Casanunda's business card: finest swordsman, most accurate crossbowman, world's second greatest lover?

16 Greebo was a pet of Nanny Ogg's. Was it a raven, a spider or a cat?

 17 What is the name of the blacksmith who produces horseshoes for Death's horse, Binky?

 18 Was the kingdom of Lancre in the Sto Plains, the Ramtop mountains or the Counterweight Continent?

 19 What is the name of the witch whose terrible singing could clean glasses and crack flowerpots?

 20 Casanunda cannot stop himself: telling the truth, being rude to others or lying?

 21 Millie Chillum is the personal maid of which witch who would become queen?

 22 King Verence II had originally been brought up to become a priest, a fool, a wizard or a soldier?

 23 Ridcully and the other wizards only have 150 dollars on them when travelling to Lancre because which one of them had eaten the key to the safe?

24 Lancre had an army of 300, 5000 or just one soldier?

25 Which old witch had, in the past, been courted by Archchancellor Ridcully?

26 What item does the small figure, Casanunda, carry to enable him to reach things that taller people can?

27 Which wizard's pointed hat contains cupboards and can form a tent?

28 Which creatures, beginning with the letter E, enter King Verence II's castle and try to capture Magrat?

29 What creature has to be given shoes made of silver, as iron shoes would kill it?

30 Do four, ten or twenty members of Unseen University take the trip to Lancre for King Verence II's wedding?

NIGHT WATCH

1 Who travels back in time and is arrested by a younger version of himself?

2 Major Clive Mountjoy-Standfast was acting commander of the cavalry during the revolution in Ankh-Morpork: true or false?

3 Mrs Palm is the head of which Guild in Ankh-Morpork: Fortune-tellers, Seamstresses or Waitresses?

4 What is the name of Lord Winder's official food taster?

5 Of the motley collection of men under Vimes's command, is Nancyball the shortest, fattest or tallest?

6 What sort of bird carries Corporal Swires into the air as part of the City Watch's work?

7 What is the name of Vimes's hero: Jacob Creasley, Jebb Haldarth or John Keel?

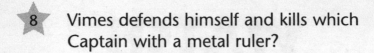

8 Vimes defends himself and kills which Captain with a metal ruler?

9 Which member of Unseen University is Head of Inadvisably Applied Magic?

10 What Lord is in charge of the Unmentionables in this book?

11 Does Lu-Tze, Miss Palm or Lord Vetinari explain to Vimes that he has been sent back in time?

12 Was Reg Shoe, Nobby Nobbs or Snouty hit by five crossbow bolts fired by Carcer and his men?

13 Vimes gave $100,000 to which doctor?

14 After Lord Winder is killed, is the new Patrician of Ankh-Morpork Lord Snapcase, Lord de Worde or Lord Vetinari?

15 Is Miss Palm's first name Jocasta, Rosie, Gemma or Sally?

16 When Vimes finally catches Carcer, how many knives has Carcer been carrying?

17 What is the name of Vimes's young son?

 18 Who killed Lord Winder?

 19 Mr Maroon is the duty porter at which Guild in Ankh-Morpork?

 20 What is the name, beginning with the letter Q, of the man Soon Shine Sun pays protection money to?

 21 Which of Vimes's constables lives in Whalebone Lane: Reg Shoe, Wiglet or Nobby Nobbs?

 22 Lady Sybil Ramkin is the wife of which member of the City Watch?

 23 Is Big Mary a siege machine, the head of the Guild of Seamstresses or the name of Lord Winder's sword?

 24 Constable Igor works for the City Watch as a jailer, as an executioner or in forensics?

 25 Carcer is made Captain of the Guard for which Patrician: Lord Winder, Lord Snapcase or Lord Vetinari?

26 What rank is Cheery Littlebottom, the female forensics staff member?

 27 When Vimes travels through time again to come back to the present day, is Captain Carrot, Nobby Nobbs or Sergeant Strongintharm the first to speak to him?

 28 Which wizard transported Vimes and Dr Lawn on his broomstick?

 29 What is the name of the female student Assassin sent at the beginning of the book to practice assassinating Commander Vimes?

 30 Snouty makes Vimes a mug of tea after he has been sleeping standing up. How long has the tea been stewing?

ERIC

1.   Which cowardly wizard can shout 'Help!' in fourteen languages?

2.   Ponce da Quirm is: an explorer, a wizard or the ruler of Klatch?

3.   What is the first name of the demon-ologist who summons up Rincewind?

4.   When a whole new universe begins, what is the first item of matter created: a single atom, a blob of goo or a paperclip?

5.   What item squashes the demon Quezovercoatl flat?

6.   How many spells make up the world: four, eight or thirteen?

7.   Tezuman are the only people who beat themselves to death with their own sui-cide notes: true or false?

8.   Do Amazonian princesses in the jungles of Klatch capture male explorers to mate with, for sacrifices or to wire plugs and put up shelves?

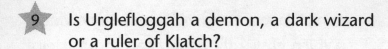

9 Is Urglefloggah a demon, a dark wizard or a ruler of Klatch?

10 Is Eric Thursley 13, 24, 55 or 87 years old?

11 Rincewind is able to plead for mercy in how many different languages?

12 What is the name of the god of mass human sacrifices in the Tezuman Empire: Offler, The Lady or Quezovercoatl?

13 Astfgl was the new king of: Klatch, the demons or the Counterweight Continent?

14 What creature keeps on saying 'Wossname'?

15 How many inches tall is the demon Quezovercoatl when he appears on Discworld?

16 Which empire depended on a buoyant obsidian knife industry: Klatch, Sto Lat or Tezuma?

17 Who tells Rincewind that Lavaeolus means 'The Rinser of Winds'?

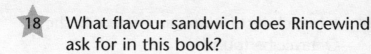

⭐ 18　What flavour sandwich does Rincewind ask for in this book?

⭐ 19　What is the name of the book that contains the spells that make up the world?

⭐ 20　Was Eric's brother, father or grandfather a demonologist?

⭐ 21　Who managed to find the Fountain of Youth and drink from it, but didn't boil the water first and died as a result?

⭐ 22　Astfgl had banned all open fires in hell: true or false?

⭐ 23　What is the name of the demon who plots the head demon's removal from power?

⭐ 24　Which demon is too old to go on a Club 18-30,000 holiday: Vassenego, Azaremoth or Urglefloggah?

⭐ 25　Who tells Eric that quantum mechanics are people who repair quantums?

26 In which institution can the book, the Octavo, be found?

 27 At the end of the book, what is the creator thinking of making from snowflakes the next day?

 28 Can animals end up in hell: yes or no?

 29 What sort of bird accompanies Rincewind and Eric through their adventures?

 30 What is the name, beginning with the letter A, of the demon also known as 'the Stench of Dog Breath'?

HOGFATHER

★1 Who gives Susan a Hogswatch card at the end of the book?

★2 Is Ridcully the Chair of Indefinite Studies, the Archchancellor or the Bursar, of Unseen University?

★3 What three letters make up the name of the computer at Unseen University?

★4 How many dollars are the Guild of Assassins offered to kill the Hogfather: 3000, 30,000, 300,000 or 3 million?

★5 The Electric Drill Chuck Key Fairy is a character mentioned in *Hogfather*: true or false?

★6 What two words, a sauce served with some roast meals, makes the Hogfather's wild boars move?

★7 Bergholt Stuttley Johnson is the Discworld's best, worst or most prolific inventor?

★8 Can you name either of the Gaiter family children that Susan is governess to?

9 Who rides the boar that turns into the Hogfather at the end of the book?

10 Is Sideney, Catseye or Medium Dave a wizard hired by Mr Teatime?

11 Can you name any of the wild boars that pull the Hogfather's sleigh?

12 When Susan meets Death and Albert as they perform the Hogfather's duties, which one had drunk 1,800,706 alcoholic drinks with no ill effect?

13 What machine writes a letter to the Hogfather asking for presents?

14 Which wizard's first name is Mustrum: Rincewind, Drum Billet or Ridcully?

15 What is the first name, beginning with the letter V, of the Tooth Fairy?

16 Hogswatchnight occurs on what date in December?

17 Bilious is the god of stale bread, hangovers or feasts?

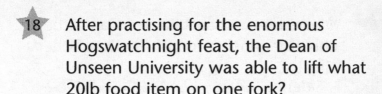

18 After practising for the enormous Hogswatchnight feast, the Dean of Unseen University was able to lift what 20lb food item on one fork?

19 Which Corporal of the City Watch tries to arrest Death dressed up as Hogfather but instead receives a top of the range crossbow as a present?

20 When Susan meets Death and Albert as they perform the Hogfather's duties, had Albert eaten 68,319 mince pies, apple pies or pork pies?

21 Which member of the Guild of Assassins spends his spare time researching how to kill Death?

22 The Duck Man is: a beggar, an evil wizard, a senior politician from Klatch or a member of the City Watch?

23 Pulling the GBL starts the Hex computer at Unseen University: what does GBL stand for?

24 What colour is the bird on the Cheerful Fairy's shoulder?

25 Where does Susan take the Gaiter children in order to visit the Hogfather's Grotto?

26 Who rescues Violet from being tied to a display case: Susan, Albert, Ridcully or Death?

27 What is Mr Teatime's first name?

28 Which character, with a first name the same as a musical instrument, does Susan order to do the Tooth Fairy's job until she returns?

29 Which one of the senior staff members at Unseen University takes dried frog pills?

30 In what form is the Hogfather when he is chased and wounded by dogs?

THE TRUTH

1 Mr Tulip believes that he will be safe as long as he has which vegetable hanging around his neck?

2 Bugarup University is in the land of Klatch, Fourecks or the Ramtops?

3 What is the name of the first printed newspaper on Discworld: *The Counterweight Courier*, *The Klatch Examiner* or *The Ankh-Mopork Times*?

4 The Patrician of Ankh-Morpork was called Lord Vetinari, Lord De Worde or Lord Selachii?

5 Copperhead is a place lived in by wizards, dwarves or trolls?

6 Does Lord de Worde, William or Mr Tulip slide a sword through the chest of Otto?

7 What is the name of the tavern that Mr Cheese owns: The Broken Drum, The Fat Fiddle or The Bucket?

8 Foul Ole Ron became the first Chief Constable, newspaper delivery boy or kebab seller in Ankh-Morpork?

9 What is the name of the zombie in *The Truth*: Mr Slant, Mr Pin or Mr Tulip?

10 Is Mr Tulip or Mr Pin an expert on antiquities?

11 The Big Wahoonie is a nickname for what city on Discworld?

12 Was Sacharissa Criplock's father an engraver, a wizard or an Assassin?

13 What is the boxer-styled name of the troll who acts as customer complaints manager at *The Ankh-Morpork Times*?

14 Mr Dibbler is the Disc's: most successful businessman, least successful businessman or an Assassin hired to kill Rincewind?

15 The semaphore towers on Discworld are known as: Flaggers, Clacks or Braggarts?

16 Which member of the *Ankh-Morpork Times* staff is a vampire: Otto, Rocky, Foul Ole Ron or William de Worde?

17 Who asks for Mr Tulip's potato, moments before killing him?

18 In Discworld, is an iconograph a sort of: telephone, camera, television or printing press?

19 Rufus Drumknott is: the Patrician's secretary, Death's manservant or the editor of *The Ankh-Morpork Times*?

20 Did William de Worde come from a wealthy family, a poor family or have no family?

21 Which member of Ankh-Morpork's City Watch turns out to be a werewolf?

22 The *Ankh-Morpork Inquirer* was the first, second or third newspaper in the city?

23 Harry King allows Goodmountain and William de Worde to steal a cart carrying what material?

24 Who disguises himself as Sister Jennifer to visit *The Ankh-Morpork Times*: Mr Slant, Mr Tulip or Mr Pin?

25 The dwarves at the printers use troll blood for red ink when printing: true or false?

26 Mr Dibbler, the sausage seller, turns out to be the main writer for *The Ankh-Morpork Inquirer*: true or false?

27 What part of William de Worde's body is injured in the fight with Mr Pin?

28 Is Gunilla Goodmountain a dwarf, troll, golem or werewolf?

29 A dog who can talk is kept by which tramp in Ankh-Morpork: Altogether Andrews, Coffin Henry or Foul Ole Ron?

30 Did Sacharissa Criplock, Rocky or Mr Bendy engrave the heading of *The Ankh-Morpork Times*?

SMALL GODS

1. What title does Vorbis hold at the start of the book: Lord, Deacon or Prophet?

2. Which character cannot read or write but listens well and has a photographic memory?

3. How many guides are there through the labyrinth of Ephebe: one, three or six?

4. Slaves in Ephebe get how many days off per week?

5. What was the name of the god who spoke to his prophet, Brutha?

6. Is Brutha, Vorbis, Sergeant Simony or General Fri'it the first to meet Death in the book?

7. What was the name of the bald, black-eyed man who led the Quisition?

8. Who is attached to the iron turtle by manacles?

9. To which country does Vorbis take Brutha: Klatch, Ephebe, Quirm or Lancre?

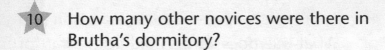

10 How many other novices were there in Brutha's dormitory?

11 When sailing to Ephebe who kills a porpoise, causing a great storm?

12 In what strangely-named year does Brutha first meet the great god, Om?

13 What is the name of the goddess of wisdom in Ephebe who appears in sculptures as a penguin?

14 At the start of the book, what animal form does the great god Om take?

15 Does Bishop Kreeblephor convert a demon using the powers of reason in the Year of the Fruitbat or the Year of the Lenient Vegetable?

16 What was the name of the secret society that wanted to overthrow Vorbis?

17 Is the biggest library anywhere on Discworld found at Unseen University, Ephebe, Klatch or the kingdom of Lancre?

18 Is his wife, nephew, son or grandson part of Didactylos's philosophy business?

19 What was the name of the country that Brutha and Vorbis came from?

20 What three word codephrase is said by Sergeant Simony and others who believe that the Discworld is flat and sits on elephants and a turtle?

21 In the desert who do the small gods try to steal Brutha from?

22 Which figure from Unseen University magically appeared to save the scrolls of Ephebe from being burnt?

23 When Om was dropped from the sky by the eagle, on whom did he land?

24 What is the name of the ship on which Vorbis chases Brutha, which is sunk by a great storm?

25 Who is ordered by Vorbis to burn down the library at Ephebe?

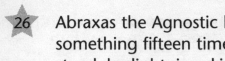 Abraxas the Agnostic had suffered something fifteen times. Was it being: struck by lightning, kidnapped or stoned by angry townspeople?

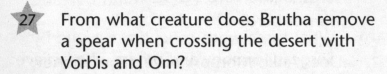 From what creature does Brutha remove a spear when crossing the desert with Vorbis and Om?

28 Who hits Brutha in the head with a rock in the desert?

29 How many eyes did the god, Om, have when in the form of a tortoise?

30 Which philosopher from Ephebe lives in a barrel and lends Brutha a book about gods?

INTERESTING
TIMES

1. What is the name of Discworld's greatest warrior hero?

2. Does Ankh-Morpork have paper money: yes or no?

3. Being beheaded is the punishment for impersonating a wizard: true or false?

4. Who challenges Lord Hong to a duel after the great battle?

5. Death introduces Rincewind to War and War's two sons. Can you name either of them?

6. What is the name of Cohen the Barbarian's group of elderly heroes aiming to overthrow the Emperor?

7. At the start of the book, a bird called a Pointless Albatross brings Ankh-Morpork a message from which empire?

8 What colour were the eyes of the goddess known as The Lady?

9 What is the name of the wizard, beginning with the letter R, who has 'Wizzard' written on his pointed hat?

10 How old was the ruthless Lord Hong: 6, 26, 86 or 366?

11 Which barbarian became Emperor of the Agatean Empire?

12 Which member of the Silver Horde was originally a geography teacher?

13 Which one of the following was not a member of the Silver Horde: Mad Hamish, Razor Henry or Truckle the Uncivil?

14 What name is given to the chest with legs that follows its owner anywhere?

15 What is the name of the book about Twoflower and his travels in Ankh-Morpork that Rincewind gets a copy of?

16 What name is given to the barrier that completely surrounds the Agatean Empire?

 17 Who is the first member of the Agatean Empire rebels that Rincewind talks to: Pretty Butterfly, One Sandal Flapping or Three Yoked Oxen?

 18 What is the name of the powerful family in Hunghung whose name begins with Mc?

 19 Which member of the Silver Horde uses swear words such as 'dang' and 'heck'?

 20 Hunghung is the capital city of which Empire?

 21 Did Cohen appoint Rincewind, Pretty Butterfly or Twoflower as Grand Vizier?

 22 Which member of the Silver Horde rode in a wheelchair: Truckle the Uncivil, Mad Hamish or Old Vincent?

 23 Which old 'friend' of Rincewind's turns out to be the father of Pretty Butterfly and Lotus Blossom?

24 Who warns Cohen that the food from the Emperor's kitchens has been poisoned by Lord Hong?

25 Can you name any of the Four Horsemen of the Common Cold?

26 Which wizard gets Dibhala to spread the rumour of the army of 2,300,009 invisible vampire ghosts?

27 Just before going into battle, Caleb gives Mr Saveloy a shield made of what food so he can eat during the fight?

28 Whose soldiers had killed Twoflower's wife: Lord Tang, Lord Sung or Lord Hong?

29 When Rincewind is sent from Unseen University to the Agatean Empire, how many guards does Cohen the Barbarian defeat in ten seconds to help him?

30 Which member of the Silver Horde was killed by a Barking Dog and was named Ronald The Apologetic by the maiden who took him to the afterlife?

MORT

1. What is the full first name of the boy who becomes Death's apprentice?

2. Who fires a crossbow bolt right through Mort: Albert, Princess Keli or Cutwell?

3. In the Mended Drum public house, is the yellow drink with wasps or the blue one with gold flecks called Spring Cordial?

4. Which character's family distilled wine from reannual grapes?

5. After Mort meets the wizard, Cutwell, which figure appears eating winkles with a pin?

6. What colour hair does Mort have?

7. How many people must Mort visit to perform Death's duties on his first night doing Death's job?

8. Is Goodie Hamstring: a thief, a witch, a writer or a midwife?

9. What is the name of the Princess that Mort has a crush on?

10 A Klatchian family sells Mort a champion racehorse that belonged to which senior figure in Ankh-Morpork?

11 What is the name of the wizard Mort meets to talk about how to walk through walls?

12 When Mort and Death fight their duel, who cheats and starts before the count of three: Mort, Death or both of them?

13 What fruit flavoured port does Goodie Hamstring offer Mort when he comes to collect her?

14 A novice is only accepted into the Listeners for training if he can hear which side a coin has landed from a distance of how many yards?

15 Is Mort's father called Lezak, Hamesh or Malich?

16 Is Klatch, Cori Celesti or the Counterweight Continent the home of the Gods?

17 What does the head of the Listeners, Abbot Lobsang, insist on doing just before he accompanies Mort?

 18 What breakfast item does Mort never dare ask Albert for: French toast, special sausages, porridge or kippers?

 19 What is the name of Wizard Cutwell's cleaning lady who comes in twice a week?

 20 Which card does Keli keep on picking from Wizard Cutwell's pack: chance, love or death?

 21 Who does Princess Keli appoint as Royal Recogniser: Mort, Cutwell or Goodie Hamstring?

 22 Miss Ysabell tells Mort that Death tried to learn to play what musical instrument once?

 23 What is the name of the extremely strong alcoholic drink Mort has in The Quene's Hed inn?

24 What colour is the Klatchian migratory bog truffle?

25 What is the name of the restaurant in which Death takes a job as a cook?

26 Nine Turning Mirrors was a vizier who attempted to kill Mort, Rincewind or the Sun Emperor?

27 What colour do Mort's eyes turn when he becomes more like Death?

28 To perform the Rite of AshkEnte, one needs 4cc of what creature's blood?

29 Who does Mort marry?

30 After the jihad that caused the deaths of 25,000 people, what additional ingredient were people allowed to add to the pizza recipe reputedly handed down by the creator?

THIEF OF TIME

1 According to Mrs War, which meat gives War wind?

2 Was Clodpool, Lu-Tze or One Hand Clapping the apprentice to Wen the Eternally Surprised?

3 What is the name of the clockmaker asked by the Auditors to make the perfect glass clock?

4 Is Lady Myria LeJean a witch, an Auditor or an Assassin?

5 Which character who appears in many Discworld novels is teaching at Madam Frout's Academy in this book?

6 What sort of bird is Quoth, who hangs out with the Death of Rats?

7 Which one of the Horsemen of the Apocalypse does Death meet in a restaurant in Genua?

8 In which city does Jeremy Clockson own a clockmaker's shop?

 9 Do the Brothers of Cool, the Balancing Monks or the Listening Monks adjust the tension of the world with small brass weights?

 10 Which guild in Ankh-Morpork raised Lobsang Ludd as a child?

 11 Which character had Lu-Tze known for almost 600 years, but in the book is currently a toddler?

 12 Procrastinators are: a type of monk, a device which can stretch time or an evil insect which eats time away?

 13 Dr Hopkins is the secretary of which Guild: the Clockmakers, Thieves or Assassins?

 14 Did Higgs & Meakins make some of the Discworld's best swords, chocolates, clocks or riding boots?

 15 Which character in the book turns out to be the son of Time?

16 What was the name of Lu-Tze's friend who offers him various gadgets including exploding sand for the journey to Ankh-Morpork?

17 Is Igor, Jeremy or Lu-Tze the first to spot that Lady LeJean's feet don't touch the ground?

18 Which of the Four Horsemen of the Apocalypse does Death meet first?

19 Who cuts off the Yeti's head?

20 Which character actually has the hands of his grandfather as his own hands?

21 Was Nanny Ogg, Magrat Garlick or Granny Weatherwax the midwife at the birth of Newgate Ludd, now known as Lobsang Ludd?

22 Which characters use human bodies to appear in Ankh-Morpork and do not normally eat?

23 Which character was also known as 'The Sweeper': Rinpo, Soon Shine Sun or Lu-Tze?

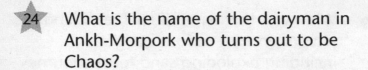

24 What is the name of the dairyman in Ankh-Morpork who turns out to be Chaos?

25 Did the Igor that worked with Jeremy Clockson come from Uberwald, Genua or Bad Ass?

26 Does Rambut Handisides work at Oi Dong Monastery, Unseen University or the Forbidden City in the Agatean Empire?

27 Who had given Death a coffee mug with the slogan 'To The World's Greatest Grandad' on it?

28 When the Auditors took human shape, did they name themselves after different fruits, animals or colours?

29 Do the red-tinted procrastinators slow time down or speed it up?

30 Which member of the History Monks is dedicated to peace as long as no one touches his hair, which is in a long ponytail?

EQUAL RITES

1. Which of the witches was offered a Chair at Unseen University?

2. What position does Cutangle hold at Unseen University?

3. What is the name of the girl, beginning with the letter E, who becomes the Disc's first female wizard?

4. What was the name of the wizard who passed on his abilities to the eighth child of Gordo Smith in Bad Ass village?

5. Which character loses his stutter at the end of the book?

6. What farmyard animal does Esk turn her brother, Gulta, into?

7. At the beginning of the book, Esk's uncontrollable magic kills a dozen of what dangerous creature?

8. What wind instrument does the god, Hoki, play badly?

9. Did Esk have three, five or seven brothers?

⭐ **10** Was Ohulan, Zemphis or Ankh-Morpork the place where Esk first met Simon?

⭐ **11** To what university does Esk try to be admitted as a student wizard?

⭐ **12** What word, beginning with the letter B, is given to Granny Weatherwax's ability to enter and ride the mind of animals?

⭐ **13** What magical object was left to Esk by Drum Billet: a staff, a wand or a pointed hat?

⭐ **14** What sort of drink does Esk ask for in the Fiddler's Riddle inn in Ohulan?

⭐ **15** What is the name of the people, beginning with the letter Z, that Esk travels with on their barges from Ohulan towards Ankh-Morpork?

⭐ **16** What household object does Esk buy to hide her wizard's staff in?

⭐ **17** What is the name of the witch Granny Weatherwax and Esk meet in Ohulan: Nanny Ogg, Magrat Garlick or Hilta Goatfounder?

18 What is the name of the wizard from Unseen University who is taking Simon to Ankh-Morpork?

19 Who manages to convince Mrs Whitlow, the housekeeper of Unseen University, to take on Esk as a maid?

20 What job did Esk's father do?

21 Which wizard joins Granny Weatherwax in the boat to search for Esk's magical staff in the river?

22 What was the name of the village that Granny Weatherwax lived in?

23 What insects build a pyramid out of sugar lumps and write in sign language the secret of longevity?

24 What item does Granny Weatherwax hurt the University porters with as she tries to approach the Archchancellor?

25 Does Unseen University eventually agree to admit girls, dwarves or trolls?

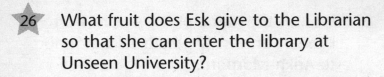 **26** What fruit does Esk give to the Librarian so that she can enter the library at Unseen University?

27 In what room at Unseen University do Granny Weatherwax and Archchancellor Cutangle have a magic duel?

28 Who does Esk's staff knock out in the library: Simon, Treatle, the Librarian or Granny Weatherwax?

29 Who starts to teach Esk the secrets of witching in Bad Ass village?

30 Nanny Annaple is a witch who had lost all her teeth by the time she was twenty, forty or sixty years old?

REAPER MAN

1 Who buys Miss Flitworth a diamond, flowers and chocolates?

2 Are mayflies, dayingales or kingtrolls the shortest living creatures on Discworld?

3 What type of tree has evolved to display its age on its trunk?

4 Which character's job is called The Duty?

5 Is Windle Poons the youngest, oldest or most deranged wizard at Unseen University?

6 The wizards of Unseen University battle against a life form in the shape of: a cash register, a lawnmower or a shopping mall?

7 Which characters, beginning with the letter A, are responsible for making Death retire?

8 Is the Tear of Offler the biggest diamond, ruby or emerald in Discworld?

9   Are the Shades the oldest, richest, newest or an invisible part of the city of Ankh-Morpork?

10   Who was given a small golden timer from Azrael as a retirement present?

11   What is the name of the club which acts as a support group for the Undead in Ankh-Morpork?

12   What vegetable do the wizards drive through Windle Poons instead of a stake?

13   What name does Death assume as he takes a job working on a farm?

14   An autocondimentor is someone who puts salt, and usually pepper, on every single meal: true or false?

15   A three-eighths Gripley is a key component of what advanced farming device?

16   Schleppel is: a vampire, a bogeyman, a shopping trolley or an ambassador from Uberwald?

17 Does Death save a little girl from a fire, an earthquake or a battle by giving her some of his time?

18 Brother Lupine is a wolf that sometimes turns into: a man, a bowl of cherries, a witch or a banshee?

19 Who is asked by Death to destroy his scythe: Mrs Cake, Iago Peedbury or Ned Simnel?

20 Which character cuts the grass in Miss Flitworth's field one stalk at a time?

21 Is the first name of the wife of the vampire Count Arthur Winkings Notfaroutoe: Elissa, Ludmilla or Doreen?

22 What does the New Death wear on his head?

23 Which female owner of a farm helps save Death from his own death?

24 Does the Dean, the Bursar or the Archchancellor start chanting 'Bonsai' and 'Yo'?

25 Was Windle Poons 90, 130, 176 or 245 when he died?

26 Who dances with Miss Flitworth all night at the Harvest Dance?

27 Who organizes the Fresh Start Club in Ankh-Morpork: Brother Lupine, Reg Shoe, Mrs Cake or One-Man Bucket?

28 What is the surname of the medium whose daughter is called Ludmilla?

29 Modo works at Unseen University, but in what position?

30 Archchancellor Ridcully states that which member of his staff has the same grasp of reality as a cardboard cut-out?

JINGO

1   Sergeant Detritus is a werewolf, an orc, a troll or a vampire?

2   What is the name of the island that emerged from the sea?

3   Is the currency of Ankh-Morpork, dollars and pence, pounds and cents or dollars and cents?

4   What title, beginning with the letter D, does the Patrician give Vimes at the end of the book?

5   Was Ashal a Colonel, a General or a Marshal in Klatch?

6   Whose wife is Lady Sybil?

7   Who organizes a game of football between the armies of Ankh-Morpork and Klatch?

8   Snowy Slopes the beheaded Assassin suffered from what hair complaint: dandruff, hair loss in patches or bright purple roots?

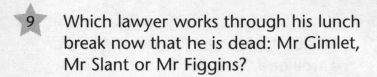

9 Which lawyer works through his lunch break now that he is dead: Mr Gimlet, Mr Slant or Mr Figgins?

10 What sort of creature is probationary constable Buggy Swires?

11 What is the name of Prince Khufurah's cultural attaché who smells strongly of cloves?

12 Ossie Brunt is an alleged Assassin, a member of the Watch or a paid spy for Klatch?

13 Which member of the faculty of Unseen University lets Carrot and Angua into the University?

14 Which member of the Watch does Lord Rust first ask to take charge after Commander Vimes is removed from authority?

15 Which Ankh-Morpork Guild earned AM$13,207,048 in a year but paid just AM$42 in tax?

★ 16 What is the name of Commander Vimes's butler, beginning with the letter W?

★ 17 Was Solid Jackson fishing for Drowning Perch, Soft Lobsters or Curious Squid when he discovered a new island?

★ 18 What is the name of Klatch's most heavily-fortified city, beginning with the letter G?

★ 19 Which member of the watch understood the Klatch language: Angua, Nobby Nobbs, Carrot or Detritus?

★ 20 What creature did Leonard of Quirm design his underwater transporter to be pulled by?

★ 21 With what country did Ankh-Morpork go to war over ownership of the island of Leshp?

★ 22 Which guild earned over AM$ 7 million but paid no taxes?

★ 23 Which member of the Ankh-Morpork Watch carries an expensive and irritating Dis-Organizer mark II?

24 What was the name of the leader of Klatch who plotted to kill his own brother?

 25 Captain Carrot provides 4000 of what item at half-time during the football match?

 26 What is the name of the overpowering perfume Corporal Nobbs buys whilst in Klatch?

 27 What is the name of the capital city of Klatch?

 28 What is the first name of Solid Jackson's son: Transparent, Half-Solid or Les?

 29 What is the name of the genius kept under control by the Patrician of Ankh-Morpork?

 30 Which Klatchian captures Angua when she is in her dog form?

WYRD SISTERS

1. What is Magrat's surname: Weatherwax, Ogg or Garlick?

2. In which kingdom does the witch Granny Weatherwax live?

3. What was the surname of the couple, beginning with the letter V, that the witches entrusted the baby boy to?

4. What is the surname of the witch with the first name, Esme?

5. Who captures Greebo the cat to lure Nanny Ogg to the castle?

6. Who is the most junior witch: Granny Weatherwax, Magrat or Nanny Ogg?

7. Do witches pay taxes in Lancre or not?

8. Does Death tell King Verence that he has to become a zombie, a troll, a priest or a ghost?

9 What is the first name given to the baby boy brought up by a band of travelling actors?

10 What relation was Felmet to the previous King of Lancre?

11 King Verence's shield is black and gold and features what animal?

12 Which of the witches holds a party on Hogswatchnight?

13 Which of the witches in the Ramtop Mountains sadly had all her own teeth and couldn't grow a wart on her face?

14 With whom does the Fool share a kiss that lasts fifteen years?

15 When Felmet asks if he sees a dagger in front of him, what does the Fool say is actually there?

16 What is the name of the dwarf who writes plays for Vitoller's actors?

17 On Hogswatchnight, who are traditionally supposed to stay at home?

18 What is the name of the theatre Vitoller is building in Ankh-Morpork?

19 Does Hwel, Tomjon or Vitoller insist on a ghost being in many of the troupe's plays?

20 What colour is Greebo, Nanny Ogg's tom cat?

21 What was the name of the King who at the start of the book is stabbed to death?

22 What is the name of the Duke who murders the King?

23 From what play does Tomjon quote when he utters his first words: *Please Yourself, The Tyrant* or *Toby Or Not Toby*?

24 What was the name of a previous King of Lancre, now a ghost, who kept the ghost of King Verence company: Sidony, Champot or Bemery?

25 Who does Tomjon rescue from a thief in Ankh-Morpork: Magrat Garlick, Hwel, The Fool or Nanny Ogg?

4

 26 Who tells Lord Felmet on the castle battlements that he is not dead, but as a result Felmet falls to the ground and dies?

 27 Who tries to release Greebo, who lands on his head and refuses to move?

 28 Who cast the spell to move the Kingdom of Lancre ahead fifteen years in time?

 29 Who is Magrat Garlick's tutor?

30 The Fool's Grandfather had won the Grand Prix des Idiots Blithering how many years in a row?

GUARDS! GUARDS!

1 Which member of the Watch bought Errol the dragon a squeaky rubber hippo?

2 True or false: Ankh-Morpork was once ruled by Giggling Lord Smince who had a Laugh-A-Minute Dungeon?

3 Cripple Mr Onion was an Assassin, a card game or a tramp?

4 Which rough member of the Watch turns out to go folk dancing on his evenings off?

5 Urdo van Pew is President of which Guild in Ankh-Morpork?

6 What creature do the Lodge of the Elucidated Brethren of the Ebon Night bring to Ankh-Morpork to scare the people who live there?

7 What type of creature does the Patrician use as spies whilst in prison?

8 What is the name of Nobby's brother, which becomes the name of the dragon given to Ankh-Morpork's Watch as a mascot?

9 Which one of the following wasn't a member of the Lodge of the Elucidated Brethren of the Ebon Night: Brother Watchtower, Brother Stent or Brother Fingers?

10 What is the name of the thief who is the first to spot the Ankh-Morpork dragon?

11 Talonthrust Vincent Wonderkind of Quirm is: a wizard, a barbarian, a dragon or a monk?

12 In his first letter back to his father how many dollars per month does Carrot say he was to get paid?

13 Lupine Wonse is whose secretary in Ankh-Morpork?

14 Apart from people who threaten the city, what other group of people will the Patrician of Ankh-Morpork not tolerate: Klatchians, dwarves or mime artists?

15 What is the name of the longest street in the city of Ankh-Morpork?

 16 Which member of the Night Watch manages to win a fight in the Mended Drum against many brawlers including Nork the Impaler, Big Henri and Grabber Simmons?

 17 What was the name of the lady whose house Carrot stayed in when he first moved to Ankh-Morpork?

 18 What is the name of the Lady who breeds swamp dragons?

 19 What is the name for adult male dragons: cocks, cobbs, cygnets or pewmets?

 20 After confronting Lupine Wonse, who is Vimes thrown in jail with?

 21 Which member of the Ankh-Morpork Watch first visited Lady Ramkin to find out about dragons?

 22 Which hapless salesman starts selling anti-dragon cream shortly after the appearance of the dragon?

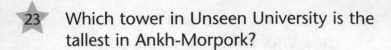

23 Which tower in Unseen University is the tallest in Ankh-Morpork?

24 Which two of these are dragon diseases: Slab Throat, Wing Mange, Dry Lung, Scale Rot?

25 Which member of the Elucidated Brethren of the Ebon Night is always sent out to get pizzas or other takeaway food: Brother Fingers, Watchtower or Plasterer?

26 Lady Ramkin identifies the plaster cast of a giant footprint that Vimes shows her as coming from *Draco nobilis*, *Draco vulgaris* or *Draco gargantua*?

27 Does Lady Ramkin live in Hard Luck Lane, Scoone Avenue or The Shades?

28 What was the name of the stolen magic book that the Librarian tells Carrot about?

29 Which member of the Watch tries to arrest the head of the Thieves' Guild?

30 The Unique and Supreme Lodge of the Elucidated Brethren of the Ebon Night planned to overthrow the Archchancellor or the Patrician of Ankh-Morpork?

THUD!

1 How many troll pieces are there in a game of Thud: 8, 16, 32 or 64?

2 What was the name of the valley where there had been fights between trolls and dwarves?

3 At what time each day does Vimes insist on reading to his young son, Sam: two o'clock, four o'clock or six o'clock?

4 Which member of the Watch suffers broken ribs when breaking up the mobs of dwarves and trolls?

5 Does the new vampire lance-constable, Sally, play the cello, the flugel horn or the bassoon?

6 Is Mr Pessimal a city department inspector, the treasurer of the Assassins' Guild or a new recruit for the Watch?

7 Did trolls, dwarves or vampires write graffiti about Mr Shine and diamonds around Ankh-Morpork?

8 On what day of the week would it be Koom Valley Day in the book?

9 What is the name of Nobby Nobbs's girlfriend who works at the Pink Pussycat Club?

10 Who told Colon and Nobbs there had been a robbery at the Royal Art Museum?

11 Who is Watch Liaison Officer: Nobby Nobbs, Fred Colon or Cheery Littlebottom?

12 What is the 'fruity' name of Vimes's Mark Five Dis-Organizer?

13 Which member of Vimes's household used to belong to the Shamlegger Street Rude Boys gang?

14 Was Otto Chriek, Doreen Winkings or John Smith, President of the Ankh-Morpork Mission of the Uberwald League of Temperance?

15 Who always buys Vimes a new Dis-Organizer whenever he gets rid of his old one?

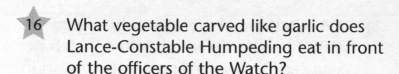

16 What vegetable carved like garlic does Lance-Constable Humpeding eat in front of the officers of the Watch?

17 How long in feet is The Battle of Koom Valley painting stolen from the Royal Art Museum?

18 Which member of the Ankh-Morpork Watch always steals the petty cash but never more than four dollars fifty?

19 What is the name of the troll in a suit that Vimes meets in the Pork Futures Warehouse?

20 Which two female members of the Watch escape from underground by reaching the Pink Pussycat Club?

21 Which officer is in charge of recruiting the Specials to the Watch: Fred Colon, Sergeant Angua or Nobby Nobbs?

22 Which creatures had a war beat called a *gahanka*?

23 A. E. Pessimal suffered what broken bone after attacking a troll?

24 What is the name of the troll, beginning with the letter B, who told the Watch he had seen a dwarf killing another dwarf in the mines?

 25 What rank is Carrot at the start of the book?

 26 Did Miss Pickles or Miss Pointer at the crystals shop lead Vimes to Mr Shine?

 27 The Summoning Dark possesses which citizen of Ankh-Morpork?

 28 Because of the way the painting was cut out of the frame, did Fred Colon surmise that the Battle of Koom Valley painting had been stolen by dwarves, trolls or vampires?

 29 How many years did it take Methodia Rascal to paint The Battle of Koom Valley?

 30 A. E. Pessimal became an acting constable as the Watch tried to defuse mobs of which two creatures from fighting each other?

GOING POSTAL

1 What was Moist von Lipwig's name on his death warrant?

2 Is Mr Groat, Mr Pump or Stanley the editor of *Total Pins* magazine?

3 Who employed Mr Gryle to burn down the Post Office?

4 Which member of the postal team dabbles in natural medicine and wears a dead mole around his neck to ward off doctors?

5 What job is Moist von Lipwig offered shortly after he is hanged to within an inch of his life?

6 What is the name of the hospital Mr Groat is taken to after the fire at the Post Office?

7 The Postmaster's hat had wings on it. Were they made of paper, clay or real pigeon's wings?

⭐ **8** Who spent 70 Ankh-Morpork dollars on a single pin at Dave's Pin Exchange?

⭐ **9** What was the name of the fearsome horse Mr Hobson gave Moist von Lipwig so that he could ride to Sto Lat?

⭐ **10** How many men had been killed in connection with the Post Office in the five weeks before Moist von Lipwig arrived?

⭐ **11** Which one of the following was not an alias used by Moist von Lipwig: Jackson McCall, Edwin Streep or Mundo Smith?

⭐ **12** Daniel 'One Drop' Trooper was to be whose executioner at the start of the book?

⭐ **13** What was the name of the man famed in Ankh-Morpork for throwing large parties including one where a troll arrived as a stripper?

⭐ **14** Who says that Moist von Lipwig has killed 2.338 people?

15 Who was called the Unfranked Man before he underwent initiation in front of the Worshipful Master?

16 Who attacked Moist von Lipwig in the burning Post Office?

17 What was the name of Moist von Lipwig's parole officer?

18 A Number Three Broad-headed Extra-Long made by Josiah Doldrum is one of the most valuable examples of what item?

19 When Senior Postman George Aggy reported for duty how many bites did he say he had received in the line of duty?

20 It costs one pence to deliver mail anywhere in Ankh-Morpork, except which part of the city where it costs five pence?

21 How much did von Lipwig charge at first for a delivery to Sto Lat: two pence, ten pence, 50 pence or one dollar?

22 Mad Al, Sane Alex and Adrian were the Smoking Gnu group who sabotaged what communications system?

 23 Whose signature does Moist von Lipwig forge on Grand Trunk company notepaper to get a reservation at Le Foix Heureux restaurant?

 24 Who tries to clean von Lipwig's suit with spot remover which removes the entire suit?

 25 After his initiation, to what position does Moist von Lipwig promote Mr Groat?

 26 What is the name of the woman von Lipwig meets the first time he visits The Golem Exchange?

 27 Apart from Mr Tiddles the cat, how many staff at the Central Post Office does von Lipwig meet on his first day?

 28 What is Groat's title at the start of the book, despite being a very elderly man?

29 Moist von Lipwig throws down a challenge to Grand Trunk, to see who can send a message faster from Ankh-Morpork to which city?

 30 What was the surname of the man that von Lipwig delivered his first letter to: Tolliver, Hugo or Parker?

MOVING PICTURES

1 What is the name of the land only thirty miles away from Ankh-Morpork where it never rains?

2 Which Guild invented moving pictures?

3 What is the name of the good looking but dim dog that comes to Holy Wood?

4 Which student wizard repeatedly fails the wizarding exams by a narrow margin?

5 What word is used to describe the films made in Discworld: clicks, clacks or cu-locks?

6 What tower at Unseen University does the giant version of Ginger climb?

7 Who becomes manager and introduces advertising to Thomas Silverfish's films?

8 Who is Victor's female co-star in his first film?

9   Deccam Ribode was: the director of United Alchemists, the last keeper of the door or the leading actor in Holy Wood films?

10   Which character becomes possessed in the book and manages to open the door in Holy Wood Hill?

11   What is the name of the talking dog who plays the harmonica badly?

12   What film, Victor's first, did Dibbler sell to the owner of The Odium picture house?

13   After being sacked by Dibbler and Silverfish, at what restaurant does Ginger begin working?

14   What was Victor Tugelbend's first film role: a troll, Cohen the Barbarian or the Patrician?

15   Which troll is employed by Dibbler and has a crush on the female troll, Ruby?

16   Which student wizard answered Victor Tugelbend's exam paper by mistake?

17 What was the name of Unseen University's brand new Archchancellor who liked jollity and staying up late at night?

 18 How many of the six imps found in the first moving picture camera Victor saw were required to blow the picture dry?

 19 Which member of Unseen University bites off a piece of the film, *Shadow of the Dessert*?

 20 Which Guild's guildhall had been rebuilt four times in two years because of explosions?

 21 From what land does an order for lots of elephants go: the Agatean Empire, Klatch, Lancre or Fourecks?

 22 Before coming to Holy Wood, did Ginger work on a farm, as an exotic dancer or as a clerk in Ankh-Morpork?

 23 What is the name of Dibbler's masterpiece, a film about civil war?

24 Was Riktor, Ridcully or Dibbler the inventor of the pot that fires lead pellets?

25 Did Ginger, Victor or Gaspode the Wonder Dog negotiate a higher fee to return to making films with Mr Dibbler?

26 Victor and Gaspode discover a giant, ancient movie theatre in what hill?

27 Thomas Silverfish is rescued from a mugging by which Unseen University student?

28 Dibbler ordered 1000 elephants for a film but he received just one other creature. What was it?

29 Who banned the making of clicks at the end of the book?

30 Whose room in Holy Wood is covered in pictures of herself?

CARPE JUGULUM

1. What is the other part of Agnes Nitt's split personality called?

2. Which of the witches is the first to be bitten by a vampire?

3. What colour are the Nac mac Feegle?

4. What was the surname of the family that Granny Weatherwax visits to try and help with a birth at the start of the book?

5. Which of Count Magpyr's servants joins the side of the witches?

6. Who is offered but declines the post of Chief Priest of Lancre?

7. Which member of the Magpyr family has a ponytail?

8. According to Nanny Ogg, what does Carpe Jugulum mean?

9 Who did Magrat originally ask to be the godmother of her child?

10 Was the first name of Magrat and the King's baby: Leanne, Esmerelda, Hermione or Agatha?

11 Who had invented draught excluders for some parts of Lancre Castle?

12 When Granny Weatherwax leaves her cottage, are all her things laid out in groups of three, five or eight?

13 When you have three witches in a coven, one is a maiden, one is a mother and what is the other called?

14 What type of bird steals Granny Weatherwax's invitation to Lancre Castle?

15 Can you name either of the two characters who get into Lancre Castle by hiding in coffins?

16 What is the mythical bird, beginning with the letter P, that Hodgesaargh is searching for?

17 What is the name of the Uberwald town, beginning with the letter E, that Vlad takes Agnes to?

18 Which short highwayman saw another highwayman killed at the start of the book?

19 Is Count de Magpyr's daughter called Morbidia, Lacrimosa or Perdita?

20 Nanny Ogg offers an island to which creatures in return for their help in protecting the kingdom against vampires?

21 Who is Lancre's Royal Historian, conductor of its Light Symphony Orchestra and operator of the Royal Mint?

22 Which of the vampires suggested Agnes chop off his head with an axe shortly after she had thrown holy water at him?

23 Who is the leader of the Nac mac Feegle that King Verence meets?

24 Granny Weatherwax insists on clinging on to what metal item after she has been bitten by a vampire?

25 What is the name of Igor's dog in Uberwald also made out of spare parts?

26 What drink do the vampire Magpyr family all start to crave?

27 Who managed to swing the axe to chop off Count de Magpyr's head?

28 The party thrown by Magrat Garlick is to celebrate: her marriage to the King, the naming of her child or the death of the tyrant?

29 What is the name of the witch living in Magrat Garlick's old cottage?

30 How many six-inch high pixies does it take to steal a full-sized cow?

SOUL MUSIC

★ 1 What stage name did Imp give himself after the band's first gig: Cliff, Buddy or Elvis?

★ 2 What colour is Susan's hair apart from a black streak down the middle?

★ 3 Which renowned unsuccessful Ankh-Morpork businessman signed up the Band With Rocks In It?

★ 4 What is the name of the troll in Imp's band?

★ 5 What was the name of the character who came from Llamedos to Ankh-Morpork with a harp?

★ 6 Which schoolfriend of Susan's was the daughter of a troll King?

★ 7 What is the name of the inn where Glod and the others are to play their first gig for five dollars?

★ 8 What is the name of the god of club musicians, beginning with the letter R?

9 Did Albert say that Susan received a My Little Binky set on her third, fifth or seventh birthday?

10 Which character surprisingly joins the Klatchian Foreign Legion?

11 Which member of the Band With Rocks In It played guitar?

12 A 64-foot long pipe organ dropped out of the sky, but from what institution had it come?

13 Which member of Unseen University had shot the Bursar with a longbow twice by accident?

14 What breakfast food does Susan order Albert to make, using Death's voice for the first time?

15 Who did Glod recruit to play keyboards for the Band With Rocks In It?

16 What was Big Mad Drongo's real name?

17 What instrument does Glod Glodsson play: guitar, drums, piano or horn?

⭐ **18** What is the name of the food establishment Binky takes Susan to where the menu offers curry with named meat for 15p as well as sweat and sour balls of pig?

⭐ **19** What is the name of the roadie hired by Mr Dibbler to help the Band With Rocks In It?

⭐ **20** Which one of the following was not a band in Ankh-Morpork which formed soon after the Band With Rocks In It: The Whom, Lead Balloon, Trollplay or Insanity?

⭐ **21** What is the name of the giant venue owned by the troll, Chrysoprase, in which the Band With Rocks In It play?

⭐ **22** Which member of Unseen University has a leather jacket with Born To Rune on the back?

⭐ **23** Who was talking to Buddy when they were summoned to Unseen University by the Rite of AshkEnte?

24 When Imp and the others visited Gimlet's Hole Food, what fried creature does Glod ask for four of?

25 What instrument did Cliff, also known as Lias Bluestone, play in the Band With Rocks In It?

26 In what town was The Jolly Cabbage inn where the Band With Rocks In It played as part of their tour?

27 Mr Cleat was: secretary of the Guild of Musicians, the promoter of the free festival in Hide Park or the bass player with Boyz In The Wood?

28 Death tells the holy man that he's seen infinity, but what colour does he tell the holy man it is?

29 Does Nobby Nobbs, Glod Glodsson or Lias Bluestone sit on and crush Imp's harp?

30 Which staff member of Quirm College For Young Ladies interviews Susan at the start of the book?

MASKERADE

1   The Opera House in Ankh-Morpork has stabling for two elephants: true or false?

2   Which ex-witch is training for a career in the opera?

3   Who turns out to be stealing money from the Opera House: Salzella, Walter Plinge or Andre?

4   What is the name of the odd-job man at the Opera House in Ankh-Morpork?

5   What item in Agnes's room in the Opera House opens to reveal a secret passage?

6   Who is the Musical Director of the Opera House at the start of the book?

7   Who does Granny Weatherwax play poker with in the cowshed with the life of a child as the stakes?

8   At the end of the book who is appointed the new artistic director of the Opera House?

9 How was Dr Undershaft killed: strangled, poisoned, knifed or shot?

10 How many dollars does Granny Weatherwax offer for Box Eight at the Opera House?

11 Which beautiful girl has to be given the lead in the operas despite the fact that she cannot sing well?

12 When Granny Weatherwax and Nanny Ogg read the tea leaves concerning Agnes what shape do the leaves take?

13 What was the name of Nanny Ogg's book on cookery which she had had published?

14 What number box is always left unsold at the Opera House on the first night of a new performance?

15 Is Mr Pounder the Opera House's organist, costume designer or rat-catcher?

16 What does the Opera House spend 1500 dollars a year on: cheese, violin strings, ballet shoes or brandy?

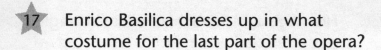

17 Enrico Basilica dresses up in what costume for the last part of the opera?

18 Was Dr Undershaft the owner, chorus master or lighting manager of the Opera House?

19 What is the name on the signed notes with lots of exclamation marks on them found at the Opera House?

20 Under what name does Enrico Basilica travel in the coach with Nanny Ogg and Granny Weatherwax?

21 What is the name of the lead role, beginning with the letter I, that Christine is to play?

22 Who helps cure the pain Death was having in his scythe arm?

23 Who is actually to sing the lead role in La Triviata whilst Christine appears to?

24 Which member of Unseen University played the organ at the Opera House?

25 After the rat-catcher, who was the next member of the Opera House to be murdered: Herr Trubelmacher, Mrs Plinge or Dr Undershaft?

26 Seldom Bucket sold what food item before getting into the opera business?

27 Did Mr Bucket, Dr Undershaft or Mr Goatberger pay Nanny Ogg $3270 for sales of her cookery book?

28 Who had won the Golden Mallet for catching the most rats for the last five years in a row?

29 Mr Gribeau, who accompanies Granny Weatherwax in the box at the Opera House, is really which animal?

30 Which one of the following was not a score of Walter Plinge's: Guys and Trolls, Miss I Gone, Miserable Les or Hubwards Side Story?

THE LAST CONTINENT

1 What was the name of the vet visiting Unseen University who assumed every patient was a racehorse?

2 What was the name of the miner, beginning with the letter S, who discovered the giant opal?

3 For what crime is Rincewind thrown in jail in Bugarup?

4 What sort of creature was Mad: a dwarf, a troll, a kangaroo or a human-like crocodile?

5 When Death asks for a list of the harmless creatures of the continent of Fourecks, what is the only creature listed?

6 At which university made of corrugated iron panels was there a tower which was half a mile high from the outside but only two storeys high from the inside?

7 What is the fruity name given to the boat discovered by the bursar which carries the wizards away from the desert island?

8 In what town in the Last Continent does Rincewind visit a bar run by a crocodile called Dongo: Dijabringabeeralong, Bugarup, Homanaway or Minogue?

9 Who hides along with Rincewind in the Luggage?

10 How many sheep was Rincewind able to shear in two minutes: half of one, one, three or thirty?

11 What sort of creature was Scrappy who talked to Rincewind: a dingo, an emu, a kangaroo or a koala bear?

12 Who was the youngest member of the faculty of Unseen University to be marooned on the desert island?

13 Is the Last Continent approximately 5000, 30,000, 100,000 or one million years old?

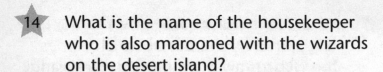 **14** What is the name of the housekeeper who is also marooned with the wizards on the desert island?

15 Which of the following trees and bushes did the wizards not find on their desert island: a cigarette tree, a pasta bush, a sherry palm, a soap bush?

16 What is the name of the character Rincewind meets who drives a wagon covered in spikes?

17 What is the name of the female impersonator Rincewind encounters who is actually a woman?

18 What contest did Rincewind win, surprisingly, after he had made a bet in Dijabringabeeralong?

19 What is the name of the mysterious white pony that carries Rincewind out of Dijabringabeeralong and that Remorse offers to buy?

20 What shortened name did Daggy and the other sheep-shearers give Rincewind?

21 Which member of Unseen University tells the other wizards about the Sledgehammer Plant of Bhangbhangduc which kills creatures with its hidden mallet?

22 Which member of Unseen University offers himself as an assistant to the god of evolution: the Bursar, the Chair of Indefinite Studies, Ponder Stibbons or the Senior Wrangler?

23 A written message on the ceiling from what outlaw allows Rincewind to escape from his cell in Bugarup?

24 Who is the first person Rincewind meets after escaping from Bugarup jail: Daggy, Fair Go Dibbler, Remorse or Archchancellor Ridcully?

25 What creature does the Librarian ward away from the wizards' boat, when he takes the form of a dolphin?

26 In what city is Rincewind forced to work in the kitchens of an opera house?

27 Which member of staff at Unseen University is very ill at the start of the book?

 28 What is the name of the Archchancellor at Bugarup University?

 29 Which member of Unseen University's office did the wizards enter and finally find a portal to a small desert island?

 30 Death has no idea as to when one character is going to die; which character is it?

PYRAMIDS

1 Which relative of Teppic's was a trained Assassin?

2 Who was the greatest storyteller ever: Copolymer, Vut, Ibid or Pythagonal?

3 What creature did Arthur attempt to sacrifice on the students' first night in Viper House?

4 Who got the Great Pyramid to flare in order to return Djelibeybi to its rightful time and dimensions?

5 The Unnamed was a smuggler's boat, owned by which of Teppic's friends?

6 What river runs through Teppic's kingdom?

7 Which creature asks Teppic a riddle, which he answers correctly with the words 'A Man'?

8 What creatures help lift Teppic up to near the top of the pyramid?

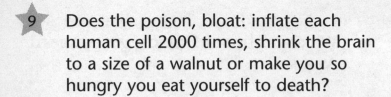

9 Does the poison, bloat: inflate each human cell 2000 times, shrink the brain to a size of a walnut or make you so hungry you eat yourself to death?

10 Who was the head priest when Teppic returned to his father's kingdom?

11 What is the name of the architect entrusted with the building of King Teppicymon XXVII's pyramid?

12 Which one of the following was not a ceremonial item King Teppic had to hold: the Cabbage of Vegetative Increase, the Staff of Certain Rains or the Flail of Mercy?

13 Can you name either of the kingdoms that Djelibeybi is sandwiched between?

14 Teppic uses his Assassin's training to rescue which handmaiden from prison?

15 What creature that Teppic and Ptraci ride happens to be the Discworld's greatest mathematician?

16 In which land does Teppic meet Endos the Listener and the philosophers, Xeno and Ibid?

17 The two philosophers are trying to prove what slow creature can outrun an arrow?

18 The mummies march to the oldest pyramid of all, but does it contain King Teppicymon XXVII, Khuft, Hoot Koomi or Dios?

19 Which member of the kingdom of Djelibeybi turns out to be 7000 years old?

20 Whose father helped Teppic sail home after the death of his father?

21 Does Lady T'malia teach Languages and Music, Codemaking, Strangulation or Political Expediency at the Assassins' Guild?

22 Which embalmer helps the king break into the pyramid of his grandmother: Dil or Gern?

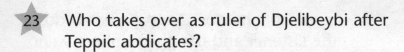

23 Who takes over as ruler of Djelibeybi after Teppic abdicates?

24 What animal killed Teppic's mother?

25 What is the ancient salute of the Assassins?

26 Teppic is diagnosed dead by a doctor even though he is alive. What animal does the doctor finally blame for his illness?

27 Which member of the Ptaclusp family was an accountant?

28 What house was Teppic in at the Assassins' Guild: Viper, Scorpion, Lizard or Shark?

29 Did Mericet teach Traps and Deadfalls, Strategy and Poison Theory or Modern Languages and Music at the Assassins' Guild?

30 Is spime, Achorion Purple or wasp agaric obtained from the liver of the inflatable mongoose?

FEET OF CLAY

1   Who is beaten to death with one of his own loaves in the Ankh-Morpork dwarf-bread Museum?

2   What earthy material is the golem, Dorfl made of?

3   Is Mr Gerhardt Sock president of the Butchers', Assassins' or Thieves' Guild in Ankh-Morpork?

4   What was the name of the priest found killed near the start of the book?

5   Which member of the Watch is rumoured to be the real Earl of Ankh?

6   Who burned down the Royal College of Heraldry: Vimes, Vetinari or Lord Downey?

7   Which owner of an iron foundry had a golem called Dibbuk which smashed itself to bits?

8   To which dwarf does Vimes give the job of head of the Forensics Department?

9   What poison does Doctor Fulsom believe has been used to poison Lord Vetinari: strychnine, arsenic, belladonna or ricin?

10   What is the name of the constable of the Watch, also a gargoyle, who guards the roof whilst Vimes looks after the ill Lord Vetinari?

11   What price has the Guild of Assassins set for Lord Vetinari's death: 10,000 dollars, 100,000 dollars or one million dollars?

12   Which member of the Watch introduced Vimes to Mr Hopkinson at the Boomerang Biscuit exhibition?

13   Which dwarf's bakery was the scene of a robbery stopped by Carrot and Angua who was in the form of a wolf?

14   How many pigeons a week is Corporal Downspout paid: one, five or twenty?

15   In which inn in Gleam Street is Angua taken hostage by three robbers?

16 What household object was filled with arsenic and was poisoning Lord Vetinari?

 17 In what sort of factory is Cheery Littlebottom saved from death by Angua in her werewolf form?

 18 Which member of the Watch turns out to be a female dwarf pretending to be a male?

 19 Who organized the poisoning of Lord Vetinari: Lord Downey, Dragon King of Arms, Mr Boggis or the dwarf, Thomas Stronginthearm?

 20 Which golem admits to the murder of Father Tubelcek even though he didn't commit the crime?

 21 A bottle of what alcohol along with a packet of arsenic was planted in Vimes's office?

 22 Which member of the Watch is invited to a party at Lady Selachii's mansion: Fred Colon, Captain Carrot or Nobby Nobbs?

23 Which member of the Watch clambers aboard Wee Mad Arthur's raft to try and escape the King Golem?

24 Igneous the troll is asked to repair which golem who becomes a member of the Watch?

25 What was Vimes doing when the first Assassin tried to kill him with a crossbow?

26 Which member of the Ankh-Morpork Watch was intending to retire shortly: Colon, Nobbs, Angua or Carrot?

27 Which member of the Watch is Dragon trying to install as leader of Ankh-Morpork?

28 Arthur Carry fires his crossbow injuring what part of Captain Carrot?

29 Mildred Easy is a missing member of the palace staff. Does she live in The Shades, Pseudopolis or the Sto Plains?

30 On hearing that he was an Earl, with which member of the Watch did Nobby Nobbs go out drinking?

WITCHES ABROAD

⭐ **1** Which one of the witches keeps the three witches' money in her knickers?

⭐ **2** Do Fairy Godmothers come in twos, threes or fives?

⭐ **3** Who rescues the witches from the dungeons they were thrown into by Lilith?

⭐ **4** Is Legba a dwarf, a frog, a cockerel or a werewolf?

⭐ **5** In which country does Desiderata Hollow live: Klatch, Sto Lat or Lancre?

⭐ **6** Which character, who shares their name with a day of the week, was once the ruler of Genua?

⭐ **7** Can you name the one piece of advice Desiderata Hollow's mother gave her about mirrors?

⭐ **8** The Duc is really what kind of animal?

9   At the end of the book, whose coronation as the ruler of Genua takes place?

 10 Against which voodoo witch does Granny Weatherwax battle and win?

 11 Who kills the snake sisters: Granny Weatherwax, Lilith, Greebo or Casanunda?

 12 How many husbands had Lady Lilith had?

 13 Who does Desiderata Hollow leave her magic wand to in her will?

 14 Lady Lilith was evil fairy godmother to: Rincewind, Ella, Mr Travis or Mrs Gogol?

 15 To what land, beginning with the letter G, do Granny Weatherwax and the other witches travel?

 16 Which of the witches wears a hat containing eighteen pockets, that could stop a blow from a hammer?

17 On their journey to Genua, the witches helped save what creatures trapped by falling rock in a mine?

 18 Which of the three witches had the first name Gytha?

 19 Who is the first person Death claims in the book?

 20 What is the name of the festival for which a grand ball is held, attended by Nanny Ogg and the other witches?

 21 In which land is it illegal to be a toymaker who doesn't whistle while he works?

 22 Which of the witches loses all of their money playing card games?

 23 What is the name of the zombie who lives with Mrs Gogol?

 24 Which one of the witches destroys the special dress Ella is supposed to wear at the ball?

 25 Who turns out to be Lady Lilith's sister?

26 Magrat Garlick turns the ceremonial coach in Genua into what vegetable?

27 Who caught and killed a vampire whilst on the journey to Genua?

28 Who uses mirrors to increase their powers?

29 Albert Hurker was the man who buried Desiderata Hollow and took a package to Magrat Garlick, but was he a soldier, a wizard, a travelling minstrel or a poacher?

30 Which one of the witches is hypnotized and dances with the Duc at the ball in Genua?

THE FIFTH ELEPHANT

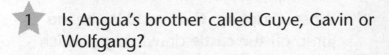

1 Is Angua's brother called Guye, Gavin or Wolfgang?

2 To which country was Vimes appointed ambassador by Lord Vetinari?

3 From what museum is the replica Scone of Stone stolen?

4 Who goes ahead of Vimes and the other members of the Watch to Uberwald because there is some trouble involving her family?

5 Which member of the Watch had become the first dwarf in Ankh-Morpork to wear a skirt?

6 What animal did the Patrician inform Vimes had been clamped by the Traffic Control part of the Watch for being parked illegally?

7 Which town in Uberwald do Vimes and the others head to, to visit the embassy?

8 Which citizen of Uberwald saved Vimes after he escaped from his cell and got trapped in a deep shaft?

9 When Gaspode, Gavin and Wolfgang jump off the castle drawbridge, which one is killed?

10 Does Vimes use a crossbow, an axe or a vial of poison to get rid of a werewolf in the boathouse after he is chased by Wolfgang and the others?

11 Lady Serafine von Uberwald was which member of the Watch's mother?

12 Who is the Ideas Taster for the Low King of Uberwald: Lady Margolotta, Dee, Gavin or Wando Sleeps?

13 Inigo Skimmer accompanies Vimes and the others as a clerk but what is his real profession?

14 Was Wallace Sonky, Leonard of Quirm or Inigo Skimmer entrusted by the Patrician to break the ciphers and codes from Uberwald?

15 Who negotiates with the Low King for fats to be shipped from Uberwald to Ankh-Morpork?

 16 Captain Carrot and Gaspode the talking dog set off towards Uberwald on the trail of Vimes, Angua or Guye von Uberwald?

 17 Regulation 301, sub-section c of the Watch's rules is to do with: officers drinking using cups and saucers, trolls on the force or the use of crossbows against thieves?

 18 Lord Vetinari talked to Sergeant Colon about the over-enthusiastic clamping of what building for causing congestion in Ankh-Morpork?

 19 Was Gavin, Guye, Garth or Growl one of the wolves in the pack that Angua had run with into Uberwald?

 20 Rhys Rhysson is the new Low King of which nation?

 21 Wolfgang von Uberwald and his pack kill which Ankh-Morpork Assassin?

22 Which of the following important people in Uberwald does Vimes make an official visit to first: the Low King, Baron von Uberwald or Lady Margolotta?

 23 Who is an agent for Ankh-Morpork: Wando Sleeps, Albrecht Albrechtsson or Captain Tantony?

 24 Which town in Uberwald has a chocolate museum in Prince Vodorny Square?

 25 Vimes dived to save the Low King of Uberwald from what item dropping from the ceiling?

 26 A mould of what object was made in Ankh-Morpork and then secretly brought to Uberwald on Vimes's coach?

 27 How many dwarves does Carrot tell Vimes now live in Ankh-Morpork: 800, 2500, 10,000 or 50,000?

 28 Who suffers a broken arm when attacking the werewolves in Uberwald: Vimes, Cheery Littlebottom, Captain Carrot or Sergeant Detritus?

29 Which troll accompanies Vimes and the others to Uberwald?

30 Who was found dead in a vat of his own liquid rubber?

MEN AT ARMS

1 Is Reg, Big Fido, Gaspode or Wowser, the Chief Barker of the Dogs' Guild?

2 Grabpot Thundergast runs a knickers, cosmetics or yoghurt factory?

3 Do trolls have hair or not?

4 Who is the richest woman in Ankh-Morpork?

5 What guild is opposite the Alchemists' Guild?

6 What is the name of the Discworld book that contains details of all the aristocracy?

7 The Sunshine Sanctuary was a place for what type of creature that was ill?

8 Who ordered Vimes to hand in his sword and was planning to disband the Night Watch?

9 What was the name of the Discworld's first ever thief who stole fire from the gods: Nick Itandrun, Fingers-Mazda or Swagman McCoy?

10 Vimes is told by Lady Sybil's lawyer that she owns about a twentieth, a tenth, a fifth or a third of Ankh?

11 Who was the last king of Ankh-Morpork?

12 Who designed the Colossus of Morpork, the Hanging Gardens of Ankh and the Quirm Memorial?

13 Is Dr Cruces the Master of Assassins, the head of the Sunshine Sanctuary or the Ambassador from Klatch?

14 How many rooms are there in Lady Sybil's mansion: 16, 34, 62 or 96?

15 Did Lord Vetinari, Lord Snapcase or Lord Rust allow the setting up of the Thieves' Guild?

16 What was the name of the dragon who exploded at the Assassins' Guild?

17 Whose main office was called The Oblong Office: the Patrician, the head of the Assassins' Guild or the head of the Thieves' Guild?

 18 Which member of the Watch befriends Gaspode the talking dog?

 19 Who was in charge of Ankh-Morpork's Day Watch?

 20 Mrs Cake's boarding house contained what sort of creature in the attic?

 21 Bundo Prung has just been expelled from the Thieves' Guild when he tries to mug which member of the Watch?

 22 When Carrot took Vimes home and sobered him up, what item had Vimes been clutching so tightly that it had cut his hand?

 23 Sergeant Colon attends which member of the Fools' Guild's funeral: Beano, Boffo or Grineldi?

24 What is the oldest Guild in Ankh-Morpork, the Thieves', Assassins', Plumbers' or Beggars' Guild?

25 What is the name of the dangerous new weapon designed by Leonard of Quirm?

26 What is the name of the female Lance-Constable who is a new recruit at the start of the book?

27 Mr Morecombe tells Vimes that Lady Sybil's estate is worth approximately how many million dollars per year?

28 Which Guild had Edward d'Eath been sent to?

29 What colour is Angua's hair when she is human?

30 Whose bedroom at the Pseudopolis Yard Watch House has absolutely no ornaments, candles, books or pictures in it?

SOURCERY

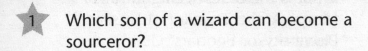

1. Which son of a wizard can become a sourceror?

2. What is the name of the sourcerer boy who impresses the wizards at Unseen University?

3. Did Creosote, Nijel or Rincewind rub the genie's lamp?

4. Does the Patrician, the Seriph, the Hermit or the Grand Poobah live in a palace called the Rhoxie?

5. What weapon does Rincewind confront Coin with: a magical sword, a dwarf battleaxe, a sock with a brick in it or a scimitar from Klatch?

6. Which Ankh-Morpork wizard was Grand Vizier Abrim battling from his tower in Klatch: Carding, Coin, Billias or Scooner?

7. Who avoided Death by jumping into his son's wizard's staff?

8. Who turns Ankh-Morpork into a modern city: Rincewind, Carding or Coin?

9 Is Spelter the Dean, the Bursar or the former Archchancellor of Unseen University?

10 How many years had Rincewind spent at Unseen University without managing to even reach level one of Wizardry?

11 Who had been decided upon as the new Archchancellor before the arrival of Coin: Spelter, Billias, Carding or Wayzygoose?

12 Which powerful wizard does Coin challenge to see his most powerful magic?

13 Who is the daughter of Cohen the Barbarian who meets Rincewind in the Mended Drum?

14 What item freezes a thief dead when it is stolen in The Shades?

15 Coin turns Lord Vetinari into what creature: a gecko, a marmoset, a snail or a baboon?

16 What ordinary job did Conina the Barbarian really want?

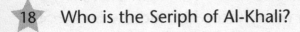

17 Did Carding, Spelter or Hakardly grab hold of Coin's staff and nearly die as a result?

18 Who is the Seriph of Al-Khali?

19 What new building does Coin build in Ankh-Morpork?

20 What item did Conina steal from Unseen University?

21 Who does Rincewind meet in the snake-pit in Al-Khali?

22 With which city does Ankh-Morpork get locked into a wizards' battle?

23 Is the Seriph's magic carpet found in the library, the treasury, the dungeons or the master bedroom?

24 To which kingdom does the Archchancellor's hat tell Conina and Rincewind to head?

25 Who lets Coin escape out of the Dungeon Dimensions but remains trapped himself?

26 Who is the wizard that Death visits at the start of the book?

 27 Which member of Unseen University goes with Rincewind and the Luggage to the Mended Drum?

 28 Into what part of Unseen University did the Librarian move all of his books?

 29 Who tried to rob the Seriph's treasury but had an asthma attack?

 30 What object caused Abrim to lose concentration and also lose the wizards' battle with Carding?

MONSTROUS REGIMENT

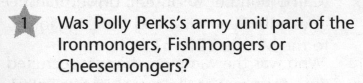

1. Was Polly Perks's army unit part of the Ironmongers, Fishmongers or Cheesemongers?

2. General Froc turns out to be: a woman, an enemy spy or a vampire?

3. Into what castle do Lieutenant Blouse and the others gain access dressed as women?

4. Does Shufti, Wazzer, Polly or Maladict become the cook for the others?

5. 'One Drop' is the slogan of vampires, trolls or ghouls who have given up killing people?

6. What was the name of Polly's lost brother?

7. Did Polly join up in the Borogravian, Zlobenian or Ankh-Morporkian army?

8 What was the name of the inn in which Polly Perks had grown up?

9 Carborundum was a troll, dwarf, banshee or zombie?

10 Who was the vampire who was recruited into the army at the same time as Polly?

11 Which one of the following was not a member of Polly's army unit: Tonker, Wazzer, Shifti or Rozzer?

12 Did Polly's army unit visit Plotz, Crotz, Drok or Ankh-Morpork first?

13 What was the name of the lieutenant who led Polly's unit to the front?

14 Can you name either of the two girls who try to become new recruits right at the end of the book?

15 Which member of Polly's unit was the first to desert?

16 Which member of the *Ankh-Morpork Times* first visited Polly's unit and took pictures of the Zlobenian prisoners?

17 Was Corporal Strappi, Captain Horentz or Lieutenant Blouse the leader of the first group of enemy soldiers that Polly and the others captured?

 18 Which member of Polly's army unit carries a wooden stake and hammer to kill vampires?

 19 Which country, beginning with the letter G, was also fighting against the Borogravians?

 20 Which sergeant in Polly's army unit knew that they were girls all along?

 21 General Froc had a food dish named after him/her. Was it the Beef Froc, the Cheese Froc, the Froc Croissant or the Froc Pie?

 22 What is the name of the Borogravian god beginning with the letter N?

 23 Against which bullying corporal does Polly practise her sword fighting skills?

24 Is Maladict, Polly, Wazzer or Lieutenant Blouse knocked out by a bag of coffee beans dropped from the air?

25 Which Lord from Ankh-Morpork makes an offer to send Polly and the others back home if they do not carry on with their attack?

26 Carborundum the troll admits that he is, in fact, a lady troll. What is her real name: Topaz, Amber or Jade?

27 Which member of the Zlobenian aristocracy is captured by Polly and her unit and gives his name as Captain Horentz?

28 What turns out to be the first name of General Froc?

29 Polly discovered Shufti was a girl on the night that who deserted their unit?

30 What drink had Maladict replaced as his craving instead of blood?

DISCWORLD

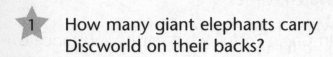
1 How many giant elephants carry Discworld on their backs?

2 What type of creature do Discworld and the elephants ride on?

3 Which character only speaks in capital letters?

4 Do the shops on Discworld open on Hogswatch Day or not?

5 What is the name of the cowardly wizard who is followed by the Luggage in a number of *Discworld* books?

6 What creature does Death ride on?

7 How many days are there in a Disc week?

8 Which university for wizards is featured in many *Discworld* books?

9 Death adopted a kitten: a girl or a boy?

10 What is the first name of the Commander of Ankh-Morpork's City Watch, Vimes?

11 In *Going Postal*, what earthy substance is Mr Pump made of?

12 In *Mort*, who, out of Albert, Miss Ysabell and Mort, can read Death's node chart?

13 What is the first name, beginning with the letter A, of Death's cook and assistant?

14 Which one of the following is not a character found in the *Discworld* books: the Electric Drill Chuck Key Fairy, the Verruca Gnome or the Baldness Troll?

15 Magrat Garlick is: a witch, an Assassin or a wizard?

16 Which member of Unseen University says, 'Oook'?

17 In *The Truth*, Mr Wintler keeps on bringing in to the newspaper office what humorously shaped objects?

18 In which city would you find Unseen University?

 19 Can anything travel faster than Discworld light?

 20 In *Guards! Guards!* Nobby Nobbs falls in love with Lady Ramkin: true or false?

 21 Whose adopted daughter is Miss Ysabell?

 22 In *Going Postal*, what is the name of the con man who introduces postage stamps?

 23 What vegetable is the principal crop of the Sto Plains?

 24 What colour are all the flowers and grass in Death's garden?

 25 What is the name of the great turtle that ferries Discworld through space?

 26 Does the River Ankh actually flow through Ankh-Morpork, Pseudopolis or through the jungles of Klatch?

27 Instead of the scythe, what weapon does Death use on kings?

28 In the book, *Hogfather*, how many wild boars draw the Hogfather's sleigh?

29 Who is summoned by the Rite of AshkEnte?

30 What is the name of Death's horse?

QUIZ 2

1 What type of young animal does Death have a fondness for?

2 In *Mort*, is Terpsic Mims out walking, fishing or drinking beer when he meets Death?

3 Is *Soul Music* set in the Century of the Fruitbat, the Century of the Yawning Tiger or the Century of the Hesitant Llama?

4 Was *The Light Fantastic*, *Sourcery* or *Equal Rites* the first Discworld novel not to feature Rincewind?

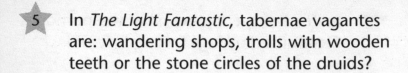

5 In *The Light Fantastic*, tabernae vagantes are: wandering shops, trolls with wooden teeth or the stone circles of the druids?

6 In *Guards! Guards!* who did the dragon that terrorized Ankh-Morpork summon for it to eat?

7 In *Thud!* is Grag Hamcrusher a dwarf, troll or golem?

8 Although he tries a number of other businesses, what is Mr Dibbler of Ankh-Morpork best known for selling in a bun?

9 Which creature from Uberwald, beginning with the letter I, is trying to breed instant fish and chips in *The Truth*?

10 In *Carpe Jugulum*, is Mightily Oats a priest, vampire, wizard or barbarian?

11 In *The Colour of Magic*, which of these is not a god: The Lady, Fortune or Chance?

12 In *Mort*, who is the first girl or woman to kiss Mort: Goodie Hamstring, Princess Keli or Miss Ysabell?

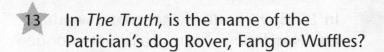

13 In *The Truth*, is the name of the Patrician's dog Rover, Fang or Wuffles?

14 In *The Last Continent*, did the Librarian, Rincewind, the Bursar or the Dean swing the bullroarer that brought rain for the first time in centuries?

15 How many miles long is the turtle, Great A'Tuin?

16 Does the Verruca Gnome first appear in *Hogfather*, *Thud!* or *Going Postal*?

17 In *Mort*, which associate of Death turned out to be the founder of Unseen University?

18 Who does Twoflower give the Luggage to at the end of *The Light Fantastic*?

19 In *Hogfather*, Mr Teatime was enrolled in which Guild?

20 What was the title of the leader of Ankh-Morpork: the Inquisitor, the Patrician or the Hogfather?

21   In *Lords and Ladies*, what metal wards off elves?

 22   In the book, *Hogfather*, who takes over the Hogfather's job?

 23   In *Carpe Jugulum*, which land do the Magpyr family come from?

 24   In *Mort*, has Abbot Lobsang been reincarnated over 20, 30 or 50 times?

 25   What rank is Carrot Ironfoundersson at the start of the book, *Men At Arms*?

 26   In *Witches Abroad*, does Saturday, Nanny Ogg or Ella squash the Duc who has been turned back into a frog?

 27   How many dwarf pieces are there in a game of Thud: 8, 16, 32 or 64?

 28   How many wizards do you need to perform the Rite of AshkEnte?

 29   In *Mort*, what does Wizard Cutwell's talking door knocker tell Princess Keli is the magic word?

30 Who pays the Guild of Assassins to kill the Hogfather?

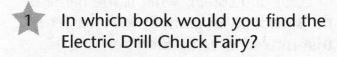
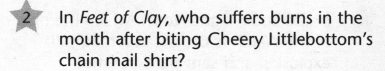
QUIZ 3

1 In which book would you find the Electric Drill Chuck Fairy?

2 In *Feet of Clay*, who suffers burns in the mouth after biting Cheery Littlebottom's chain mail shirt?

3 In *The Truth*, is Mr Pin's partner Mr Tulip, Lord Vetinari or Mr Dibbler?

4 In *Going Postal*, who goes to see Professor Pelc about the strange events in the Post Office?

5 In Ankh-Morpork, how many types of cheese are there: 50, 125, 250 or 1500?

6 In *Mort*, Miss Ysabell says she has been what age for 35 years?

7 In *Interesting Times*, Three Solid Frogs is: an artist, a taxman or a guard?

8   In *The Truth*, is the name of the character who confesses to every crime that occurs in Ankh-Morpork: Done It Duncan, Ted the Confessor or Accused Alan?

 9   In *Lords and Ladies*, what is the name of the kingdom, beginning with the letter L, that is ruled over by King Verence II?

 10   In the book *Night Watch*, which member of the Watch is caught in a magical explosion and sent back in time?

 11   In *Pyramids*, what Guild does Teppic belong to before leaving Ankh-Morpork to become ruler of the kingdom of Djelibeybi?

 12   In *Mort*, who does job broker, Liona Keeble, say has no marketable skills?

 13   In *Interesting Times*, do the gods say that the Hongs, the Tangs or the Sungs were the most powerful family on the Counterweight Continent?

 14   In *Mort*, what is the name of the tavern in which Death tries to get drunk?

15 In *The Colour of Magic*, is Tethis a dragon, a god or a sea troll?

16 What was the shortened first name, beginning with the letter S, of the first vampire to join Ankh-Morpork's Watch?

17 In *Mort*, is the drink scumble made from berries, apples, pigswill or sour milk?

18 In *Thud!* which member of the Watch has the nickname, amongst dwarves, of Head Banger?

19 At the start of the book *Hogfather*, Susan kills a monster with how many legs?

20 In *Men At Arms*, does the first bullet from the Assassin in the tower hit Lord Vetinari, Corporal Carrot or Angua?

21 What was the name of the first ever tourist on Discworld?

22 In *Going Postal*, what meaty food is the traditional offering to Offler the Crocodile God?

23 In *Interesting Times*, Rincewind is befriended by the Emperor of which empire?

 24 In *Mort*, which relative of Princess Keli's attempted to kill her before he was bumped on the head by Cutwell?

 25 What kingdom is cut off from the rest of Discworld by the Lancre River?

 26 In *The Light Fantastic*, who gave Cohen the Barbarian a bag of gold as a wedding gift?

 27 What mythical creature did Jason Ogg have to fit horseshoes to at the end of the book *Lords and Ladies*?

 28 Can you name either of the main directions in which the Discworld turns?

 29 Can you name two of the sports that Susan Sto-Helit was good at at school?

 30 In *Mort*, does Princess Keli live in Ankh-Morpork, Sto Lat or Klatch?

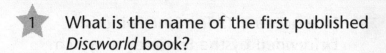

1 What is the name of the first published *Discworld* book?

2 In *The Last Continent*, in what city is Rincewind forced to work in the kitchens of an opera house?

3 In *Hogfather*, which character rides on Death's horse to reach the Castle of Bones?

4 What is the name of the evil murderer of many people in the book *Night Watch*?

5 How many levels of wizardry are there on Discworld?

6 In *The Truth*, what is the name of the Editor of the Disc's first newspaper?

7 In *Soul Music*, who took over Death's duties whilst he was away: Susan, Mort or Albert?

8 In *Mort*, which surprising uninvited guest to the Patrician's tenth anniversary party does a conga-like dance holding on to Lord Rodley?

9 True or false: in *The Last Continent*, Rincewind eats a meat pie covered in pea soup and tomato sauce?

10 In *The Colour of Magic*, what is the name of the tourist from the Agatean Empire that Rincewind has to look after?

11 In *Mort*, are Mellius and Gretelina billed as the world's greatest rivals, lovers or friends – even though they were born 200 years apart and on different continents?

12 In which book would you find the criminal characters Chickenwire, Medium Dave and Banjo Lilywhite?

13 In *The Truth*, what is the name of the steeplejack who always pretends to jump from buildings: Harry King, Arthur Crank or Augustus Periwinkle?

14 What is unusual about the biography books in Death's library?

15 In *Guards! Guards!* who is chained to a rock in the centre of a plaza wearing a nightie and rubber boots?

16 In *Mort*, when Princess Keli calls at Wizard Cutwell's, is she first offered: Shield of Passion ointment, Ramrub or Belladonna eyedrops?

17 Which member of the Watch was told at the age of sixteen that he wasn't a dwarf but was a human?

18 The ring of stones in Lancre in the book *Lords and Ladies* is called the Pillars, the Monoliths or the Dancers?

19 In *The Colour of Magic*, who owns The Broken Drum inn: Broadman, Bravd the Hublander or Weasel?

20 Is the 25th Discworld book: *Thud!*, *The Truth* or *Going Postal*?

21 In *The Light Fantastic*, who is Chancellor of Unseen University: Mustrum Ridcully, Galder Weatherwax or Werdholm Jelt?

22 Was Lord Mountjoy Quickfang Winterforth IV a vampire, a dragon, a zombie or a wizard?

23 Lord Downey was the head of which Guild in Ankh-Morpork?

 24 In *The Truth*, Corporal Nobbs turns out to be the dog informer, Deep Bone: true or false?

 25 In *Mort*, is Old Overcoat the name of a tramp, a tavern in Ankh-Morpork or a type of drink served at The Mended Drum?

 26 In *Lords and Ladies*, who is Magrat engaged to be married to?

 27 Who performs their first proper spell in *The Light Fantastic*?

 28 In *Thud!*, what is the name of the book that Commander Vimes reads to his son Young Sam every evening?

 29 In *Witches Abroad*, which cat is turned into a human by the witches to foil Lady Lilith's plans?

30 In *Men At Arms*, who gets married at the end of the book?

1 In *Mort*, who does Mort stop from being assassinated in her bedroom?

2 The Listeners were Discworld's youngest, largest, oldest or smallest religious sect?

3 What large animal was a feature of Princess Keli's coronation in the book *Mort*?

4 In *Moving Pictures*, what film do the wizards of Unseen University flock to see in Ankh-Morpork?

5 In *The Colour of Magic*, Twoflower's big gold coins are called hagash, rhinu or baggadosh?

6 Foul Ole Ron sells what newspaper in *The Truth*?

7 In *Mort*, what oath is the first thing Death says?

8 In *The Thief of Time*, is the fourth surprise Lobsang Ludd discovers in the Garden of Five Surprises: a yodeling stick insect, poisonous daisies or the bronze butterfly?

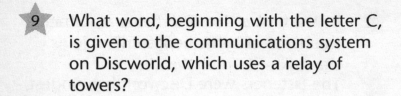 **9** What word, beginning with the letter C, is given to the communications system on Discworld, which uses a relay of towers?

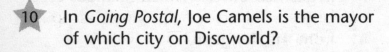 **10** In *Going Postal*, Joe Camels is the mayor of which city on Discworld?

11 What is the name of the student wizard in charge of the Hex computer at Unseen University?

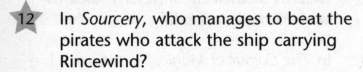 **12** In *Sourcery*, who manages to beat the pirates who attack the ship carrying Rincewind?

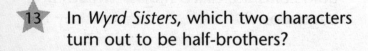 **13** In *Wyrd Sisters*, which two characters turn out to be half-brothers?

14 In *Carpe Jugulum*, who is given a potion by pixies and becomes a frenzied fighting machine?

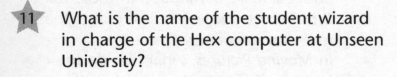 **15** In *The Last Continent*, is Rincewind reunited with his luggage in Bugarup, Dijabringabeeralong, Worralorrasurfa or back in Ankh-Morpork?

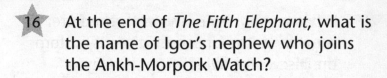

16 At the end of *The Fifth Elephant*, what is the name of Igor's nephew who joins the Ankh-Morpork Watch?

17 In *Guards! Guards!* which member of Unseen University helps Vimes escape from the dungeon?

18 What is the name given to plants that grow backwards in time?

19 In *Mort*, does Mort's, Albert's or Miss Ysabell's biography fill a whole shelf in Death's library?

20 In *Men At Arms*, which dwarf and acting constable in the Watch was killed by the Assassin?

21 What type of buildings or rooms are all connected together in L-space?

22 In *Mort*, Death took part in Cripple Wa's crap game using three dice. How many sides did each of the dice have?

23 Did Albert, Death or Cutwell set fire to the bursar's beard in *Mort*?

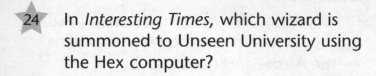

24 In *Interesting Times*, which wizard is summoned to Unseen University using the Hex computer?

25 Which character was so skilled as a blacksmith that he had once put shoes on an ant?

26 In *Men At Arms*, which member of the Assassins' Guild does Lord Downey put a ten thousand dollar bounty on: Dr Cruces, Beano Fibkins, Edward d'Eath or Earl Creosote?

27 In which Terry Pratchett book does Death ride a sleigh and give children presents?

28 At the end of the book *Interesting Times*, does Rincewind end up in Unseen University, the Counterweight Continent or the land called XXXX?

29 In *Mort*, how old was Princess Keli when she was supposed to be assassinated?

30 In *Thief of Time*, who is sent to Jeremy Clockson in a crate as an assistant?

ANSWERS

THE COLOUR OF MAGIC

1. Elbows
2. Rincewind
3. Liartes
4. The edge of the Rim
5. Berilia
6. Eight
7. The Assassins' Guild
8. The Disc's gods
9. A dragon
10. Black
11. Great T'Phon
12. 800 days
13. A direction that Discworld turns in
14. Hrun the Barbarian
15. Four
16. Black Oroogu
17. Twoflower
18. Wyrmberg
19. Icy
20. Slight breezes
21. The Soul-Eater
22. Rincewind
23. Laolith, Psepha
24. Hrun the Barbarian
25. Rincewind's
26. Eight
27. Sunlight
28. Krull
29. He had his eyes put out
30. Jerakeen

THE LIGHT FANTASTIC

1. The Tower of Art
2. A poet
3. Bethan
4. A Thaum
5. Ymper Trymon
6. Cohen the Barbarian
7. Rincewind
8. Beryl
9. The Dean of Liberal Studies
10. Ysabell
11. The Bumper Fun Grimoire
12. 64 signs
13. A computer hardware consultant
14. Ymper Trymon
15. The Forest of Skund
16. Ysabell
17. The Luggage
18. Death
19. Cohen the Barbarian
20. A broomstick
21. The Celestial Halibut
22. The oldest
23. Twoflower
24. Twoflower
25. The Smarl
26. A dwarf
27. The Lawnmower
28. Trymon
29. Three
30. Illustrious Mage of the Five Kingdoms

LORDS AND LADIES

1. Rejected
2. Lancre
3. Elves
4. A pumpkin
5. Bees
6. Magrat Garlick
7. Weighs almost a kilo per coin
8. Offler the Crocodile God
9. Mountains
10. 200 dollars
11. Granny Weatherwax
12. True
13. Nanny Ogg

14. Ridcully, Ponder Stibbons, the Bursar, the Librarian
15. Finest swordsman, world's second greatest lover
16. A cat
17. Jason Ogg
18. The Ramtop mountains
19. Nanny Ogg
20. Lying
21. Magrat Garlick
22. A fool
23. The Bursar
24. One soldier
25. Granny Weatherwax
26. A stepladder
27. Ridcully's
28. Elves
29. Unicorn
30. Four

NIGHT WATCH

1. Vimes
2. True
3. Seamstresses
4. Spymould
5. Tallest
6. A heron
7. John Keel
8. Captain Swing
9. Ponder Stibbons
10. Lord Winder
11. Lu-Tze
12. Reg Shoe
13. Dr Lawn
14. Lord Snapcase
15. Rosie
16. Four
17. Sam Jr
18. Havelock Vetinari
19. The Guild of Assassins
20. Corporal Quirke
21. Reg Shoe

22. Vimes
23. A siege machine
24. In forensics
25. Lord Snapcase
26. Corporal
27. Captain Carrot
28. Ridcully
29. Jocasta Wiggs
30. An hour

ERIC

1. Rincewind
2. An explorer
3. Eric
4. A paperclip
5. The Luggage
6. Eight
7. True
8. To wire plugs and put up shelves
9. A demon
10. 13 years old
11. Twelve
12. Quezovercoatl
13. The demons
14. The parrot
15. Six inches
16. Tezuma
17. Eric
18. Egg and cress
19. The Octavo
20. Grandfather
21. Ponce da Quirm
22. True
23. Vassenego
24. Urglefloggah
25. Rincewind
26. Unseen University
27. Alphabet Snow
28. Yes
29. A parrot
30. Azaremoth

ANSWERS

HOGFATHER

1. Death
2. Archchancellor
3. Hex
4. 3 million
5. True
6. Apple sauce
7. Worst inventor
8. Gawain, Twyla
9. Susan
10. Sideney
11. Snouter, Tusker, Gouger, Rooter
12. Albert
13. The Hex computer
14. Ridcully
15. Violet
16. 32nd December
17. Hangovers
18. A turkey
19. Corporal Nobbs
20. Pork pies
21. Mr Teatime
22. A beggar
23. Great big lever
24. Blue
25. The Maul
26. Susan
27. Jonathan
28. Banjo
29. The Bursar
30. A boar

THE TRUTH

1. A potato
2. Fourecks
3. *The Ankh-Morpork Times*
4. Lord Vetinari
5. Dwarves
6. Lord de Worde
7. The Bucket
8. First newspaper delivery boy
9. Mr Slant
10. Mr Tulip
11. Ankh-Morpork
12. An engraver
13. Rocky
14. Least successful businessman
15. Clacks
16. Otto
17. Mr Pin
18. A camera
19. The Patrician's secretary
20. A wealthy family
21. Sergeant Angua
22. The second
23. Paper
24. Mr Tulip
25. False
26. True
27. His arm
28. A dwarf
29. Foul Ole Ron
30. Sacharissa Criplock

SMALL GODS

1. Deacon
2. Brutha
3. Six
4. One
5. Om
6. General Fri'it
7. Vorbis
8. Brutha
9. Ephebe
10. 23
11. Vorbis
12. The Year of the Notional Serpent
13. Patina
14. A tortoise
15. The Year of the Lenient Vegetable

16. The Turtle Movement
17. Unseen University
18. His nephew
19. Omnia
20. The Turtle Moves
21. Om
22. The Librarian
23. Vorbis
24. The Fin of God
25. Brutha
26. Struck by lightning
27. A lion
28. Vorbis
29. One
30. Didactylos

INTERESTING TIMES

1. Cohen the Barbarian
2. No
3. True
4. Twoflower
5. Terror and Panic
6. The Silver Horde
7. The Agatean Empire
8. Green
9. Rincewind
10. 26
11. Cohen the Barbarian
12. Ronald Saveloy
13. Razor Henry
14. The Luggage
15. *What I Did On My Holidays*
16. The Great Wall
17. Pretty Butterfly
18. McSweeney
19. Mr Saveloy
20. The Agatean Empire
21. Twoflower
22. Mad Hamish
23. Twoflower
24. Rincewind
25. Chesty, Nostril, Lack of Tissues, Sniffles

26. Rincewind
27. Chocolate
28. Lord Hong
29. Five
30. Mr Saveloy

MORT

1. Mortimer
2. Cutwell
3. The yellow drink with wasps
4. Mort's
5. Death
6. Red
7. Three
8. A witch
9. Princess Keli
10. The Patrician
11. Igneous Cutwell
12. Both of them
13. Raspberry port
14. 1000
15. Lezak
16. Cori Celesti
17. Shouting as loud as he can
18. Porridge
19. Mrs Nugent
20. Death
21. Cutwell
22. The banjo
23. Scumble
24. Brown (pale brown)
25. Harga's House of Ribs
26. The Sun Emperor
27. Blue
28. A mouse
29. Miss Ysabell
30. A small bay leaf

THIEF OF TIME

1. Beef
2. Clodpool
3. Jeremy Clockson

4. An Auditor
5. Susan
6. A raven
7. Famine
8. Ankh-Morpork
9. The Balancing Monks
10. The Thieves' Guild
11. The Abbot
12. A device which can stretch time
13. The Clockmakers' Guild
14. Chocolates
15. Lobsang Ludd
16. Qu
17. Igor
18. Pestilence
19. Lu-Tze
20. Igor
21. Nanny Ogg
22. The Auditors
23. Lu-Tze
24. Ronald Soak
25. Uberwald
26. Oi Dong Monastery
27. Susan
28. Colours
29. Speed it up
30. Marco Soto

EQUAL RITES

1. Granny Weatherwax
2. Archchancellor
3. Esk (Eskarina)
4. Drum Billet
5. Simon
6. A pig
7. Wolves
8. The flute
9. Seven brothers
10. Zemphis
11. Unseen University
12. Borrowing

13. A staff
14. Goat's milk
15. Zoons
16. A broomstick
17. Hilta Goatfounder
18. Treatle
19. Granny Weatherwax
20. A blacksmith
21. Cutangle
22. Bad Ass
23. Ants
24. A hatpin
25. Girls
26. A banana
27. The Great Hall
28. Simon
29. Granny Weatherwax
30. Twenty

REAPER MAN

1. Death
2. Mayflies
3. The Counting Pine
4. Death
5. The oldest
6. A shopping mall
7. Auditors
8. The biggest diamond
9. Oldest
10. Death
11. The Fresh Start Club
12. Celery
13. Bill Door
14. True
15. A Combination Harvester
16. A bogeyman
17. A fire
18. A man
19. Ned Simnel
20. Death
21. Doreen
22. A crown

23. Miss Flitworth
24. The Dean
25. 130
26. Death
27. Reg Shoe
28. Cake
29. Gardener
30. The Senior Wrangler

JINGO

1. A troll
2. Leshp
3. Dollars and pence
4. Duke
5. General
6. Commander Vimes's
7. Captain Carrot
8. Dandruff
9. Mr Slant
10. A gnome
11. 71-Hour Ahmed
12. An alleged Assassin
13. The Librarian
14. Captain Carrot
15. The Guild of Assassins
16. Willikins
17. Curious Squid
18. Gebra
19. Carrot
20. Dolphins
21. Klatch
22. The Guild of Accountants
23. Commander Vimes
24. Prince Cadram
25. Oranges
26. Kasbah Nights
27. Al Khali
28. Les
29. Leonard of Quirm
30. 71-Hour Ahmed

WYRD SISTERS

1. Garlick
2. Lancre
3. Vitoller
4. Weatherwax
5. Felmet
6. Magrat
7. No
8. A ghost
9. Tomjon
10. His cousin
11. Bears
12. Nanny Ogg
13. Granny Weatherwax
14. Magrat Garlick
15. A handkerchief
16. Hwel
17. Witches
18. The Dysk Theatre
19. Hwel
20. Grey
21. King Verence
22. Duke Felmet
23. *The Tyrant*
24. Champot
25. The Fool
26. Death
27. The Fool
28. Granny Weatherwax
29. Goody Whemper
30. Four

GUARDS! GUARDS!

1. Carrot
2. True
3. A card game
4. Nobby Nobbs
5. The Guild of Thieves
6. A dragon
7. Rats
8. Errol
9. Brother Stent

10. Zebbo Mooty
11. A dragon
12. Twenty
13. The Patrician's
14. Mime artists
15. Short Street
16. Carrot
17. Rosie Palm
18. Lady Ramkin
19. Cobbs
20. The Patrician
21. Vimes
22. Cut me own Throat Dibbler
23. The Tower of Art
24. Slab Throat, Dry Lung
25. Brother Fingers
26. *Draco nobilis*
27. Scoone Avenue
28. *The Summoning of Dragons*
29. Carrot
30. The Patrician of Ankh-Morpork

THUD!

1. 8
2. Koom Valley
3. Six o'clock
4. Commander Vimes
5. The cello
6. A city department inspector
7. Trolls
8. Saturday
9. Tawneee
10. Sir Reynold Stitched
11. Fred Colon
12. The Gooseberry
13. The butler, Willikins
14. John Smith
15. His wife, Lady Sybil
16. A radish
17. Fifty feet
18. Nobby Nobbs
19. Chryoprase

20. Sally and Angua
21. Fred Colon
22. The trolls
23. A broken arm
24. Brick
25. Captain
26. Miss Pointer
27. Commander Vimes
28. Trolls
29. Sixteen
30. Dwarves and trolls

GOING POSTAL

1. Albert Spangler
2. Stanley
3. Reacher Gilt
4. Mr Groat
5. Postmaster General of Ankh-Morpork
6. Lady Sybil Free Hospital
7. Real pigeon's wings
8. Moist von Lipwig
9. Boris
10. Four
11. Jackson McCall
12. Moist von Lipwig
13. Reacher Gilt
14. Mr Pump
15. Moist von Lipwig
16. Mr Gryle
17. Mr Pump
18. A pin
19. Fifteen
20. The Shades
21. Ten pence
22. The Clacks
23. Reacher Gilt's signature
24. Mr Pump
25. Postal Inspector
26. Adora Belle Dearheart
27. Two
28. Junior Postman

29. Genua
30. Parker

MOVING PICTURES

1. Holy Wood
2. The Guild of Alchemists
3. Laddie
4. Victor Tugelbend
5. Clicks
6. The Tower of Art
7. Cut Me Own Throat Dibbler
8. Ginger Withel
9. The last keeper of the door
10. Ginger
11. Gaspode the Wonder Dog
12. *Sword of Passione*
13. Borgle's
14. Cohen the Barbarian
15. Detritus
16. Ponder Stibbons
17. Ridcully
18. Four
19. The Librarian
20. The Guild of Alchemists
21. Klatch
22. On a farm
23. *Blown Away*
24. Riktor
25. Gaspode the Wonder Dog
26. Holy Wood Hill
27. Victor Tugelbend
28. A camel
29. The Patrician
30. Ginger Withel

CARPE JUGULUM

1. Perdita
2. Granny Weatherwax
3. Blue
4. Ivy
5. Igor
6. Mightily Oats

7. Vlad
8. Go for the Throat
9. Granny Weatherwax
10. Esmerelda
11. Shawn Ogg
12. Three
13. A crone
14. A magpie
15. Mightily Oats and Agnes Nitt
16. Phoenix
17. Escrow
18. Casanunda
19. Lacrimosa
20. Pixies
21. Shawn Ogg
22. Vlad
23. Big Aggie
24. An anvil
25. Scraps
26. Tea
27. Mightily Oats
28. The naming of her child
29. Agnes Nitt
30. Four

SOUL MUSIC

1. Buddy
2. White
3. Cut Me Own Throat Dibbler
4. Lias Bluestone
5. Imp (Imp y Celyn)
6. Princess Jade
7. The Mended Drum
8. Reg
9. Her third birthday
10. Death
11. Imp (Buddy)
12. Unseen University
13. The Archchancellor
14. A boiled egg
15. The Librarian
16. Adrian Turnipseed

ANSWERS

17. Horn
18. Curry Gardens
19. Asphalt
20. Trollplay
21. The Cavern
22. The Dean
23. Susan
24. Fried rats
25. Rocks
26. Scrote
27. The secretary of the Guild of Musicians
28. Blue
29. Lias Bluestone
30. Miss Butts

MASKERADE

1. True
2. Agnes Nitt
3. Salzella
4. Walter Plinge
5. The mirror
6. Mr Salzella
7. Walter Plinge
8. Death
9. Strangled
10. Two thousand dollars
11. Christine
12. The shape of a skull
13. *The Joye of Snacks*
14. Number eight
15. Rat-catcher
16. Ballet shoes
17. A chicken costume
18. The chorus master
19. The Opera Ghost
20. Henry Slugg
21. Iodine
22. Granny Weatherwax
23. Agnes
24. The Librarian
25. Dr Undershaft

26. Cheese
27. Mr Goatberger
28. Mr Pounder
29. Greebo the cat
30. Miss I Gone

THE LAST CONTINENT

1. Doughnut Jimmy
2. Strewth
3. Sheep stealing
4. A dwarf
5. Sheep (some of them)
6. Bugarup University
7. The melon boat
8. Dijabringabeeralong
9. Neilette
10. Thirty
11. A kangaroo
12. Ponder Stibbons
13. 30,000 years old
14. Mrs Whitlow
15. A sherry palm
16. Mad
17. Neilette
18. A sheep-shearing contest
19. Snowy
20. Rinso
21. Ponder Stibbons
22. Ponder Stibbons
23. Tinhead Ned
24. Fair Go Dibbler
25. Sharks
26. Bugarup
27. The Librarian
28. Bill Rincewind
29. The Professor of Cruel and Unusual Geography
30. Rincewind

PYRAMIDS

1. Uncle Vyrt
2. Copolymer

3. A goat
4. Teppic
5. Chidder
6. The Djel
7. The Sphinx
8. Mummies
9. Inflates each human cell 2000 times
10. Dios
11. Ptaclusp
12. The Staff of Certain Rains
13. Tsort and Ephebe
14. Ptraci
15. A camel
16. Ephebe
17. A tortoise
18. Khuft
19. Dios
20. Chidder's father
21. Political Expediency
22. Gern
23. Ptraci
24. A crocodile
25. A thumb pressed up against the first two fingers
26. A walrus
27. Ptaclusp IIa
28. Viper House
29. Strategy and Poison Theory
30. Spime

FEET OF CLAY

1. Mr Hopkinson
2. Clay
3. The Butchers' Guild
4. Father Tubelcek
5. Nobby Nobbs
6. Vimes
7. Thomas Stronginthearm
8. Cheery Littlebottom
9. Arsenic
10. Constable Downspout

11. One million dollars
12. Captain Carrot
13. Mr Ironcrust
14. Five
15. The Bucket
16. Candles
17. A candle-making factory
18. Cheery Littlebottom
19. Dragon King of Arms
20. Dorfl
21. Whiskey
22. Nobby Nobbs
23. Fred Colon
24. Dorfl
25. Shaving
26. Colon
27. Nobby Nobbs
28. His hand
29. The Shades
30. Fred Colon

WITCHES ABROAD

1. Nanny Ogg
2. Twos
3. Casanunda
4. A cockerel
5. Lancre
6. Saturday
7. Never stand between two of them
8. A frog
9. Ella's
10. Mrs Gogol
11. Greebo
12. Three
13. Magrat Garlick
14. Ella
15. Genua
16. Nanny Ogg
17. Dwarves
18. Nanny Ogg
19. Desiderata Hollow

20. Samedi Nuit Mort
21. Genua
22. Nanny Ogg
23. Saturday
24. Magrat Garlick
25. Granny Weatherwax
26. A pumpkin
27. Greebo
28. Lady Lilith
29. A poacher
30. Magrat Garlick

THE FIFTH ELEPHANT

1. Wolfgang
2. Uberwald
3. The Dwarf Bread Museum
4. Angua
5. Cheery Littlebottom
6. A duck
7. Bonk
8. Lady Margolotta
9. Gavin
10. An axe
11. Sergeant Angua
12. Dee
13. Assassin
14. Leonard of Quirm
15. Lady Sybil
16. Angua
17. Officers drinking using cups and saucers
18. The Opera House
19. Gavin
20. Uberwald
21. Inigo Skimmer
22. The Low King
23. Wando Sleeps
24. Bonk
25. A chandelier
26. The Scone of Stone
27. 50,000
28. Captain Carrot

29. Detritus
30. Wallace Sonky

MEN AT ARMS

1. Big Fido
2. Cosmetics
3. They do not
4. Lady Sybil Ramkin
5. The Gamblers' Guild
6. Twurp's Peerage
7. Dragons
8. Lord Vetinari (the Patrician)
9. Fingers-Mazda
10. A tenth
11. King Lorenzo the Kind
12. Bloody Stupid Johnson
13. Master of Assassins
14. 34
15. Lord Vetinari
16. Chubby
17. The Patrician
18. Angua
19. Captain Quirke
20. A banshee
21. Angua
22. His badge
23. Beano
24. The Beggars' Guild
25. A gonne
26. Angua
27. Seven
28. The Assassins' Guild
29. Blonde
30. Sam Vimes

SOURCERY

1. The eighth son
2. Coin
3. Nijel
4. The Seriph
5. A sock with a brick in it
6. Carding

7. Ipslore the Red
8. Coin
9. The Bursar
10. Sixteen years
11. Wayzygoose
12. Billias
13. Conina
14. The Archchancellor's hat
15. A gecko
16. A hairdresser
17. Carding
18. Creosote
19. The Tower of Sourcery
20. The Archchancellor's hat
21. Nijel the Barbarian
22. Al-Khali
23. The treasury
24. Klatch
25. Rincewind
26. Ipslore the Red
27. The Librarian
28. The Tower of Art
29. Nijel the Barbarian
30. The Luggage

MONSTROUS REGIMENT

1. Cheesemongers
2. A woman
3. Kneck Keep
4. Shufti
5. Vampires
6. Paul
7. Borogravian
8. The Duchess
9. A troll
10. Maladict
11. Rozzer
12. Plotz
13. Lieutenant Blouse
14. Mary, Rosemary
15. Corporal Strappi
16. Otto Chriek
17. Captain Horentz
18. Igor (Igorina)
19. Genua
20. Sergeant Jackrum
21. The Beef Froc
22. Nuggan
23. Corporal Strappi
24. Maladict
25. Lord Rust
26. Jade
27. Prince Heinrich
28. Mildred
29. Strappi
30. Coffee

DISCWORLD QUIZ 1

1. Four
2. A giant star turtle
3. Death
4. No
5. Rincewind
6. A horse
7. Eight
8. Unseen University
9. A girl
10. Samuel (Sam)
11. Clay
12. Miss Ysabell
13. Albert
14. The Baldness Troll
15. A witch
16. The Librarian
17. Vegetables
18. Ankh-Morpork
19. Yes
20. False
21. Death's
22. Moist von Lipwig
23. Cabbages
24. Black
25. Great A'Tuin
26. Ankh-Morpork

27. A sword
28. Four
29. Death
30. Binky

DISCWORLD QUIZ 2

1. Kittens
2. Fishing
3. The Century of the Fruitbat
4. *Equal Rites*
5. Wandering shops
6. Lady Sybil Ramkin
7. Dwarf
8. Sausages
9. Igor
10. Priest
11. Fortune
12. Goodie Hamstring
13. Wuffles
14. Rincewind
15. 10,000
16. *Hogfather*
17. Albert
18. Rincewind
19. The Guild of Assassins
20. The Patrician
21. Iron
22. Death
23. Uberwald
24. Over 50 times
25. Corporal
26. Saturday
27. 32
28. Eight
29. Please
30. The Auditors

DISCWORLD QUIZ 3

1. *Hogfather*
2. Angua
3. Mr Tulip
4. Moist von Lipwig

5. 1500
6. Age 16
7. An artist
8. Done It Duncan
9. Lancre
10. Vimes
11. The Assassins' Guild
12. Death
13. The Hongs
14. The Mended Drum
15. Sea troll
16. Sally
17. Apples
18. Carrot
19. Eight
20. Lord Vetinari
21. Twoflower
22. Sausages
23. The Agatean Empire
24. Her uncle
25. Lancre
26. Twoflower
27. A unicorn
28. Hubward, Rimward
29. Hockey, lacrosse, rounders
30. Sto Lat

DISCWORLD QUIZ 4

1. *The Colour of Magic*
2. Bugarup
3. Susan
4. Carcer
5. Eight
6. William De Worde
7. Susan
8. Death
9. True
10. Twoflower
11. Greatest lovers
12. *Hogfather*
13. Arthur Crank
14. The books wrote themselves

15. Lady Sybil Ramkin
16. Shield of Passion ointment
17. Carrot
18. The Dancers
19. Broadman
20. *The Truth*
21. Galder Weatherwax
22. A dragon
23. The Assassins' Guild
24. False
25. A type of drink served at The Mended Drum
26. King Verence II
27. Rincewind
28. *Where's My Cow?*
29. Greebo
30. Vimes and Lady Sybil Ramkin

DISCWORLD QUIZ 5

1. Princess Keli
2. Oldest
3. An elephant
4. *Blown Away*
5. Rhinu

6. *The Ankh-Morpork Times*
7. OH BUGGER
8. A yodeling stick insect
9. Clacks
10. Sto Lat
11. Ponder Stibbons
12. Conina
13. The Fool and Tomjon
14. King Verence II
15. Bugarup
16. Igor
17. The Librarian
18. Reannuals
19. Albert's
20. Cuddy
21. Libraries
22. Eight
23. Albert
24. Rincewind
25. Jason Ogg
26. Edward d'Eath
27. *Hogfather*
28. The land called XXXX
29. Fifteen
30. Igor